Personal and Professional Development

EFFECTIVE
TEAMWORK

Michael A. West

Professor of Work and Organizational Psychology
Institute of Work Psychology
University of Sheffield

 Published by The British Psychological Society

First published in 1994 by BPS Books (The British Psychological Society),
St Andrews House, 48 Princess Road East, Leicester LE1 7DR.

© Michael A. West, 1994.

A catalogue record for this book is available from the British Library.

ISBN 1 85433 138 8 paperback

Typeset by Gem Graphics, Trenance, Mawgan Porth, Cornwall
Printed in Great Britain by BPC Wheatons Ltd, Exeter

EFFECTIVE

97004729

RK

Michael A. West

04 10
13

This book is due for return on or before the last date shown below.

Don Gresswell Ltd., London, N.21   Cat. No. 1207   DG 02242/71

EFFECTIVE
TEAMWORK

Michael A. West

Personal and Professional Development

SERIES EDITORS:

Glynis M. Breakwell is Professor of Psychology and Head of the Psychology Department at the University of Surrey.

David Fontana is Reader in Educational Psychology at University of Wales College of Cardiff, and Professor Catedrático, University of Minho, Portugal.

The books in this series are designed to help readers use psychological insights, theories and methods to address issues which arise regularly in their own personal and professional lives and which affect how they manage their jobs and careers. Psychologists have a great deal to say about how to improve our work styles. The emphasis in this series is upon presenting psychology in a way which is easily understood and usable. We are committed to enabling our readers to use psychology, applying it for themselves to themselves.

The books adopt a highly practical approach. Readers are confronted with examples and exercises which require them to analyse their own situation and review carefully what they think, feel and do. Such analyses are necessary precursors in coming to an understanding of where and what changes are needed, or can reasonably be made.

These books do not reflect any single approach in pschology. The editors come from different branches of the discipline. They work together with the authors to ensure that each book provides a fair and comprehensive review of the psychology relevant to the issues discussed.

Each book deals with a clearly defined target and can stand alone. But combined they form an integrated and broad resource, making wide areas of psychological expertise more freely accessible.

OTHER TITLES IN THE SERIES

ACKNOWLEDGEMENTS

I am grateful to Marie Hughes for tolerating my tapes and for her kindness and support; to those in the team from which I learn most – Rebecca Lawthom, Malcolm Patterson, Julie Slater and David Staniforth; to the many teams with whom I have worked and learned and whose experience I have leaned upon to write this book; and to the present and former postgraduate students with whom I have studied teams and whose ideas and applied organizational work have been sources of learning and creative conflict, especially David Bunce, Caroline Burningham, Josephine Hennessy, Tracey Hepplestone, Indrihadi Isnaeni, Stephen Kellet, Nigel King, Brenda Poulton, Patricia Sullivan and Michael Stead. Finally, my thanks to those whose teachings and writings have most influenced the contents of this volume: Gillian Hardy, Serge Moscovici, Nigel Nicholson and Sogyal Rinpoche.

Contents

DEDICATION TO

Gillian

Nikolaos   Rosa   Thomas

Eleanor

INTRODUCTION

At the basis of human society, of the family and of all social functioning is the question of how people can combine their efforts and imaginations to work in ways which enhance the quality of life through the achievement of certain goals. Indeed the major challenges which face our species today require answers to the question: 'How can we live and interact in ways which maximize the quality of life for all people while, at the same time, sustaining the resources offered by the planet?' These are also the major problems in Personal and Professional Development: i.e. how effective collaboration can be achieved in practice.

This book does not offer a simple list of solutions to the problems of working together and interacting effectively since there is no easy way of creating effective teams. The world in which we live changes too rapidly for any single set of prescriptions to be adequate. Change is endemic and this demands flexible individuals, flexible teams and flexible organizations, if they are to be effective and survive.

What this book does suggest is that teams, like individuals, have to reflect upon their functioning and adapt in ways which are appropriate to their changing circumstances. Such an orientation requires:

- intelligent scanning of the environment;
- awareness of the functioning of the team;
- flexibility or readiness to change;
- tolerance of ambiguity and difference within the team;
- a preparedness to accept uncertainty as change occurs.

One reason why simple prescriptions cannot be offered for effective team work is that teams operate in varied organizational settings as diverse as multi-national oil companies, voluntary organizations, health care organizations and religious institutions. While team effectiveness is an important issue in all, the people who constitute these teams are likely to differ in personality and background.

Even within organizations teams differ markedly. Increasingly within Europe, for example, teams are constituted from people who have different cultural backgrounds. In some organizations teams may span national boundaries, including perhaps members located in a number of different nation states, all of whom are required to work effectively together. Moreover, changes in work patterns such as part-time, flexitime, contract and home working all add further mixes to the heterogeneity of teams. As teams become more diverse in their constitution and functioning, team members must learn to reflect upon, and intelligently adapt to, their constantly changing circumstances in order to be effective. This is the simple but powerful message of this book for those who wish to develop effective team functioning.

TASK AND SOCIAL ELEMENTS OF TEAM FUNCTIONING

There are two fundamental dimensions of team functioning: the task the team is required to carry out, and the social factors which influence how members experience the team as a social unit. The basic reason for the creation of teams in work organizations is the expectation that they will carry out tasks more effectively than individuals and so further organizational objectives overall. Consideration of the content of the task, and the strategies and processes employed by team members to carry out that task, is important for understanding how to work in teams. At the same time, teams are composed of people who have a variety of emotional, social and other human needs which the team as a whole can either help to meet or frustrate.

In order to function effectively, team members must actively focus upon their objectives, regularly reviewing ways of achieving them and the team's methods of working. At the same time, in order to promote the well-being of its members, the team must reflect upon the ways in which it provides support to members, how conflicts are resolved and what is the overall social climate of the team - or its 'social reflexivity'. The purpose of these review processes should be to provide active steps to change the team's objectives, ways of working or social functioning, in order to promote effectiveness.

But what does 'team effectiveness' mean? In this book, team effectiveness is seen as having three main components:

1. Task effectiveness is the extent to which the team is successful in achieving its **task-related objectives**.

2. **Mental health** refers to the well-being, growth and development of team members.

3. **Team viability** is the probability that a team will continue to work together and function effectively.

Figure 1 shows the two elements of teams, the task and social elements, drawn together to illustrate four extreme types of team functioning and the likely effects upon the three principal outcomes of team functioning: task effectiveness, team members' mental health and team viability.

**High
Task
Reflexivity**

Type D: Cold Efficiency Team High task effectiveness Average or poor mental health Short term viability	*Type A: Fully Functioning Team* High task effectiveness Good mental health Long term viability
Low Social Reflexivity	**High Social Reflexivity**
Type C: Dysfunctional Team Poor task effectiveness Poor mental health Very low team viability	*Type B: Cosy Team* Poor task effectiveness Average mental health Short term viability

**Low
Task
Reflexivity**

Figure 1: Four types of teams and their outcomes

Type A, the *Fully functioning team*, represents a team which is high in both task and social reflexivity, i.e. the extent to which the team reflects on and modifies its objectives, processes, task and social support strategies appropriately in changing circumstances. Such teams are likely to be characterized by high levels of mental health amongst team members, high task effectiveness and sustained viability, i.e. they are likely to be able to and want to continue to work together over a period of time.

Type B, the *Cosy team*, represents teams high in social reflexivity and low in task reflexivity. This is a team where there is a good deal of warmth, support and cohesion amongst team members, but where the ability to get the task done effectively is rather low. Therefore, while mental health will tend to be good and people will feel very positive towards the team, the organization's satisfaction with team performance will be low. As a result its viability will be threatened, although team members may well wish to continue to work together over a period of time. To some extent mental health may be adversely affected by the low levels of competence experienced by team members in a team which is minimally task effective.

Type C, the *Dysfunctional team*, is the worst scenario where a team is low on both task and social reflexivity. Such teams will have very low viability since team members will be dissatisfied with both interpersonal relationships and with the sense of achievement and quality of task functioning experienced.

Finally team type D, the *Cold efficiency team*, is a team in which task reflexivity tends to be high, but where the social functioning of the team is poor. Within such teams, task performance will generally be good, but the team viability and mental health of members will be adversely affected by the poor social functioning of the team. Team members will not wish to stay working in a group which they perceive as providing little social support and which is characterized by a poor social climate.

These two aspects of team functioning, i.e. task and social reflexivity, have a direct impact upon the three principal outcomes of team functioning - task effectiveness, team members' mental health and team viability. In this book we shall examine these elements of team functioning and describe practical ways in which team reflexivity can be enhanced by consideration of the principal aspects of team work:

➤ team objectives

➤ participation in teams

➤ task orientation

➤ support for innovation.

Team social functioning will also be explored in relation to four areas:

➤ social support within the team

➤ team climate

➤ team support for growth and well-being

➤ methods of conflict resolution.

Throughout, we shall address the basic question: 'How can people work most effectively together in teams?'

EXERCISE 1

To measure levels of task and social reflexivity in your team, ask all your team colleagues to complete this questionnaire without consulting each other about the answers. Add the scores for task reflexivity and social reflexivity separately, i.e. add all team members' scores for the task element and then all team members' scores for the social element. Divide both totals by the number of people completing the questionnaire. At the bottom of this box are values against which you can determine whether your team's scores are high, low or average compared with the scores of other teams. Indicate how far each statement is an accurate or inaccurate description of your team by writing a number in the box beside each statement, based on the following scale of 1 to 7:

Very inaccurate 1	2	3	4	5	6	Very accurate 7

(a) **Task reflexivity**
1. The team often reviews its objectives. ☐
2. We regularly discuss whether the team is working effectively together. ☐
3. The methods used by the team to get the job done are often discussed. ☐
4. In this team we modify our objectives in light of changing circumstances. ☐
5. Team strategies are rarely changed. ☐
6. How well we communicate information is often discussed. ☐
7. This team often reviews its approach to getting the job done. ☐
8. The way decisions are made in this team is rarely altered. ☐
   Total score ☐

(b) **Social reflexivity**
1. Team members provide each other with support when times are difficult. ☐

─ continued ─

continued– –

2. When things at work are stressful the team is not very supportive. ☐
3. Conflict tends to linger in this team. ☐
4. People in this team often teach each other new skills. ☐
5. When things at work are stressful, we pull together as a team. ☐
6. Team members are often unfriendly. ☐
7. Conflicts are constructively dealt with in this team. ☐
8. People in this team are slow to resolve arguments. ☐

Total score ☐

	(a) Task reflexivity	(b) Social reflexivity
High scores	42–56	48–56
Average scores	34–41	40–47
Low scores	0–33	0–39

Chapter One

Do Teams Work?

ARE TEAMS MORE EFFECTIVE THAN INDIVIDUALS WORKING ALONE?

It is precisely because human beings have learned to work co-operatively together that we have made such astonishing progress as a species. When we work co-operatively we can accomplish infinitely more than if we work individually. This is the principle of synergy – that the whole is greater than the sum of its individual parts.

In many areas of human activity and endeavour, research has shown how group working can lead to greater efficiency or effectiveness. In hard rock mining, the introduction of group goals led to greater quantity of rocks mined. In work safety studies, the introduction of group goals and training saw an increase in safe work behaviour. In a study of timber harvesting, the introduction of group goals led to a higher output rate. In a study of restaurant services, the introduction of group working for staff was associated with higher customer ratings of service quality, comfort and cleanliness. In an insurance company, increased compliance with a 24 hour reporting standard was found after the introduction of group working. And in truck loading and unloading, truck turnaround time was reduced after the introduction of a group goal.

The list goes on, including tasks as diverse as solving anagrams; refurbishing donated household goods for resale; building Tinker toy structures; and raising money for voluntary organizations. Indeed, if we pause and consider the way most aspects of our social life are structured, group work is often the underlying structure. And not without good reason. It is by working together and pooling our resources (abilities, experience, time, money etc.) that we can most effectively accomplish our shared goals.

However, although group working is very effective, it is important to know how to work effectively in groups. Our educational systems often emphasize individual working almost to the exclusion of group working. Consequently, the skills of working in groups have to be learned and developed. There are many barriers to effective group working which group members must overcome if they are to succeed in achieving synergy – the added advantage of working in groups over and above the outputs from individuals working alone. It is to a description of these barriers that we now turn.

BARRIERS TO EFFECTIVE TEAMWORK

In the 1890s a French agricultural engineer, Max Ringelmann, attempted to discover whether individuals working alone were more effective than people working in groups. He instructed agricultural students to pull on a rope attached to a dynamometer and measured the amount of pull. Working alone, the average student could pull a weight of 85 kg. Ringelmann then arranged the students in groups of seven and instructed them to pull on the rope as hard as possible. The average pull for a group of seven was 450 kg. The groups were pulling only 75% as hard as the aggregated work of seven individuals pulling alone.

Further research has involved groups solving cognitive problems such as how to transport sheep and wolves safely across a river in a single boat. It showed that although groups took longer than individuals, overall they did better in achieving correct solutions. Other tasks involved '20 questions' games. Here a particular object is selected and players have to guess the name of the object by asking up to 20 questions, to which they are given only a 'yes' or 'no' answer. Groups were slightly more effective than individuals in getting the correct solution within their 20 questions, but were much less efficient in terms of time use. Individuals took, on average, 5 person minutes to come up with the correct solution. Groups of two took 7 person minutes (i.e. 3.5 minutes in real time) and groups of four, 12 person minutes (3 minutes in real time). There were no differences between groups of two and four in the likelihood of them getting correct answers.

Why do these effects occur? They seem to result from a phenomenon which social psychologists call 'social loafing'. Social loafing refers to the fact that individuals work less hard when their efforts are combined with those of others, than when they are considered individually. When people are in teams where their work is less identifiable and cannot easily be evaluated, they simply make less effort. This is not to say that all we have to do is single out those who 'socially loaf'. Rather, it is a characteristic of human behaviour that people work less hard in groups than if they alone were responsible for task outcomes.

Recently the Ringelmann experiments have been replicated by other researchers. In one example the person at the front of a rope was instructed to pull on the rope and was told that there were six people behind them also pulling. Each person pulling was blind-folded and so was unable to see what was going on behind them. In some cases the other 'pullers' simply stood behind the person at the front and made grunting noises suggesting that they were pulling when they were, in reality, making no effort. When individuals *believed* that they were in groups of seven pulling on the rope, they pulled with only 75 percent of the effort they made when they were working individually. In another devious social psychological experiment, the researcher instructed individuals to shout as loud as they could, either alone or, as they were told, in groups. They were blind-folded and given ear defenders to cut out visual and sound cues. When people believed they were shouting with others, they exerted only 74 percent of the effort that they made when they believed they were shouting alone.

These difficulties of social loafing, therefore, present real and particular problems for working in groups. They also challenge the common assumption that 'synergy' is produced by individuals working in groups, i.e. the idea that teams are more effective than the sum of the contributions of individual members. In such cases, 1 + 1 + 1 + 1 does not necessarily produce five; in many cases, 1 + 1 + 1 + 1 may produce three.

GROUP PROBLEM-SOLVING AND DECISION-MAKING

The social loafing explanation of poor group performance is help-ful in understanding some of the difficulties faced by groups. However, it does not account for the fact that group decision-making is sometimes inexplicably flawed. For example, in 1952,

Maier and Solem presented groups with mathematical questions. They deliberately formed some groups which had an individual in them who knew how to work out the answers. Surprisingly, they found that many of the groups still failed to come up with the correct solutions. Why should this be?

Although we tend to think of groups as somehow reasonable and logical they are greatly influenced by hierarchical considerations. In most primary health care teams for example, the opinions of the doctors in a meeting will have much greater influence than the opinions of the receptionists. Because of superior status, the doctor exerts more influence over the thinking of the group. Group leaders tend to have more influence over decisions regardless of whether their views are correct or incorrect. Moreover, dominant personalities within groups exert a disproportionate influence over group outcomes. Studies of jury decision-making have shown that it may be the person who talks most who has most influence over the jury verdict.

BASEBALL OR BASKETBALL TEAMS?

In an interesting example of the importance of individual accountability for team work, some researchers in the United States attempted to predict the performance of baseball and basketball teams at the end of a season from ratings of the abilities of individual team members. Each team member was given a score from 1 to 10 to denote overall ability within their professional sport. These were then added together and used to predict the eventual performance of a team over a whole season. In one sport the aggregated ratings of the individual abilities of team members predicted team performance with 90% accuracy, while in the other sport, they predicted with only 35% accuracy.

Which do you think was which?

(*The answer to this question is given over page along with an explanation for the finding.*)

Overall, the research indicates that in many kinds of tasks the performance of teams is about 75 percent as effective as the performance of the aggregate of individuals working alone. Moreover, in relation to quality of decision-making, research suggests that group performance is generally superior to that of the average member of the group, but often inferior to that of its most competent individual.

BRAINSTORMING IN GROUPS

Another assumption about group working in organizations is that groups promote greater creativity than do individuals working alone. It is thought that individuals will spark one another's creativity into flame and that, as a result, there will be many more excellent ideas produced. This is such a widely-held assumption that when I have challenged it within certain organizations, many managers have argued vehemently against me. What is the research evidence about group creativity?

Early studies comparing the effectiveness of brainstorming individually or in groups involved creating 'statisticized' and 'real' groups. Statisticized groups (groups consisting of people who never actually work together, but whose performance is based on the statistical addition of their individual efforts) consisted of five individuals working alone in separate rooms who were given a five-minute period to generate ideas on uses for an object. Their results were aggregated at the end and any redundant ideas due to repetition by different individuals were taken out. Real groups of five individuals worked together for five minutes generating as many ideas as possible and withholding criticism. The statisticized groups produced an average of 68 ideas, while the real groups produced an average of only 37 ideas.

In over 20 studies conducted since 1958, this finding has almost always been confirmed. Individuals working alone produce more ideas when they are aggregated than do groups working together. Many managers immediately argue that the quality of ideas produced by groups will be better than the quality of ideas produced by individuals. However, the research does not support this conclusion either. Most measures indicate that individuals working alone produce superior quality ideas (i.e. in numbers of good ideas), and there is no research evidence suggesting that groups produce superior quality. In short, individuals working alone produce a greater quantity of ideas, and ideas of at least as good quality as in brainstorming groups.

Why should groups fail to produce the synergistic outcomes that we expect of them in brainstorming groups? The explanation appears to be that when people are speaking in brainstorming groups other individuals are not able to speak and so are less likely to put ideas forward. Moreover, they are busy holding their ideas in their memories, waiting for a chance to speak, and this interferes with their ability to produce other ideas. Furthermore, people may feel inhibited from offering what they see as a relatively ordinary idea after a particularly creative idea has been offered by another group member.

BASEBALL OR BASKETBALL TEAMS?

The result (see page 4)
It was possible to predict baseball team scores with 90% accuracy since team performance is much more dependent upon individual performance in batting and pitching. Basketball involves passing, co-ordination and team strategies for scores. Individual accountability is greater in baseball therefore and this makes it easier to predict team performance.

Accepting the fact that production blocking and other factors can inhibit performance of brainstorming groups, it is still argued that there are three important reasons for working in group settings when proposing new ideas and new ways of doing things. The first reason is that those who make up teams in 'real life' as opposed to laboratory settings, have valuable experience of the particular domains of the team's work. For example, in a primary health care team, there are people with nursing, medical and social work backgrounds. Together they bring a broad range of important experience to the team's deliberations. It is important that team members are involved in the brainstorming process, so that this wide experience is available as a resource.

The second reason for brainstorming in groups is the importance of participation. Involving all those affected by organizational change in the process of change is vital in order to gain commitment and reduce resistance. Working in brainstorming groups, especially where the groups are focusing on ideas for change, encourages commitment to that process. Finally, many team members argue that it is just more fun to brainstorm in groups, and that humour and laughter are outcomes which themselves can spur creativity.

Despite these arguments it is clear from the research that the mechanics of the process can be usefully altered to overcome the production blocking effect. Group members should brainstorm individually to generate their own ideas before bringing them to the group. Then each member should have the opportunity to present all of his or her ideas to the group before evaluation and selection takes place.

BUILDING AN EFFECTIVE TEAM

How can teams at work overcome some of the problems which have been identified so far such as social loafing? Although the research described has not been encouraging about the superiority of team work over individual work, nevertheless some very clear guidelines can be offered for increasing group effectiveness.

GROUPS SHOULD HAVE INTRINSICALLY INTERESTING TASKS TO PERFORM

A good deal of research evidence indicates that people will work harder if the tasks they are asked to perform are intrinsically interesting, motivating, challenging and enjoyable. Where people are required to fit the same nut on the same bolt hour after hour, day after day, they are unlikely to be motivated and committed to their work. Where teams have an inherently interesting task to perform there is generally high commitment, higher motivation and more co-operative working. This therefore calls for very careful design of the objectives and tasks of work groups (see Chapter 2).

In many companies influenced by Japanese management practices, individuals work in relatively autonomous self-managing teams, re-designing work themselves to make tasks more meaningful and to improve quality of performance. Teams should be given tasks which are intrinsically interesting, but should also be given considerable autonomy in modifying task objectives to ensure that the team's goals help to maintain overall motivation.

INDIVIDUALS SHOULD FEEL THEY ARE IMPORTANT TO THE FATE OF THE GROUP

Social loafing effects are most likely to occur when people believe that their contributions to the group are dispensable. For example, in working with primary health care teams, my colleagues and I have found that some members feel their work is not highly valued. Health visitors and receptionists are particularly likely to feel this way. One way that individuals can come to feel that their work is important to the fate of the group is through the use of techniques of *role clarification* and *negotiation*. These are described more fully in Chapter 8. By careful exploration of the roles of each team member, together with the identification of team and individual objectives, team members can see and demonstrate more clearly to other team members the importance of their work to the success of the team overall.

INDIVIDUALS SHOULD HAVE INTRINSICALLY INTERESTING TASKS TO PERFORM

Individual tasks should also be meaningful and inherently rewarding. Just as it is important for a group to have an intrinsically interesting task to perform, so too will individuals work harder, be more committed and creative if the tasks they are performing are engaging and challenging. For example, a researcher sitting in on team meetings and observing team processes is more motivated and has a more creative orientation towards the task, than the researcher who is required to input the data from questionnaires on to a computer.

INDIVIDUAL CONTRIBUTIONS SHOULD BE INDISPENSABLE, UNIQUE AND EVALUATED AGAINST A STANDARD

Research on social loafing indicates that the effect is considerably reduced where people perceive their work to be indispensable to the performance of the team as a whole. Equally important, however, is that individual work should be subject to evaluation. People have to feel that not only is their work indispensable, but also that their performance is *visible* to other members of the team. In laboratory settings, where team members know that the products of their performance will be observed by other members of the team, they are much more likely to maintain effort to the level which they would achieve normally in individual performance. For example, when individuals are told that each team member's shouting will be measured to assess individual contribution to the overall loudness of the team, the classic social loafing effect does not occur. Therefore, it is important within team settings for each team member to feel that their performance will be evaluated against a standard within the group, at the end of some specified period of team performance. For a general practitioner this might be measured by such things as: the number of surgery patients seen; the quality of clinical interactions with patients;

patient satisfaction with the general practitioner; the number of home visits completed; the quality of clinical interactions during home visits; prescribing practices; and the quantity and quality of communications with other team members.

THERE SHOULD BE CLEAR TEAM GOALS WITH BUILT-IN PERFORMANCE FEEDBACK

For the same reasons that it is important for individuals to have clear goals and performance feedback, so too is it important for the team as a whole to have clear group goals with performance feedback. Research evidence shows very consistently that where people are set clear targets to aim at, their performance is generally improved. However, goals can only function as a motivator of team performance if accurate performance feedback is available. For example, in the case of primary health care teams, there should be performance feedback at least annually on all or some of the following indices:

- patient satisfaction with the quality of care given;

- effectiveness of innovations and changes introduced by the team;

- quality of clinical care given in the team;

- improvement in community health;

- the effectiveness with which they have achieved their own objectives as a team;

- quality of team climate and how well team members feel they have worked together;

- quality of intra-team communication;

- quality of relationships with other agencies such as social services, local authority and hospitals;

- financial effectiveness of the practice;

- efficiency of the practice in reducing patient waiting times;

- improvement in patient access to health care and health promotion.

The more precise the indicators of team performance, the more likely a team is to improve its performance and inhibit the effects of social loafing.

MEASURING THE EFFECTIVENESS OF YOUR TEAM'S PERFORMANCE

EXERCISE 2

1. Identify all those groups or important individuals who have an interest or 'stake' in your team's work: These might include:

   - management
   - customers
   - service receivers
   - other teams/groups in your organization
   - those in other organizations
   - the general public
   - you and your team colleagues.

2. Identify the criteria of effectiveness each of these 'stakeholders' might use to evaluate your team's effectiveness. Taking those listed under 1 above, these might include:

   - meeting the organization's objectives
   - providing quality goods on time and giving good 'after sales service'
   - providing a helpful, timely, excellent and considerate service
   - giving useful information
   - co-operating effectively
   - producing goods or services of value to society, in an ethical way
   - having a good quality of working life and experiencing a sense of growth and development.

   (These criteria can be made much more detailed for your team and each stakeholder will probably have a number of other criteria.)

3. Give a rating from 1 (*not at all important*) to 7 (*of great importance*) to each criterion. If possible ask other team members to do the same. This can be useful for identifying areas of agreement and disagreement.

- - continued

continued —

4. Give a rating from 1 (*not at all effective*) to 7 (*highly effective*) on each criterion in terms of how well you feel the team is achieving on each criterion. Again, if possible, your colleagues should go through a similar rating process. This exercise will give a simple but clear indication of how well you feel the team is achieving in each area. By subtracting the 'effectiveness' score from the 'importance' score you will also get a good indication of areas where action appears most urgently needed to improve performance.

PERSONALITY AND TEAM PERFORMANCE

Experience of working in teams suggests that personalities play an important part in the effectiveness of teams working together. The questions often raised are:

'What types of people work best together?'

'What sort of mix of personalities is needed for a team to be effective?'

'In what ways must group members be compatible in order to work together effectively?'

Not surprisingly, team members' overall ability is linked to group performance. This was well demonstrated in one study of military crews which showed that people of high ability contributed most to performance when all the other crew members were also high in ability. It appears that talent is used more effectively when it is concentrated rather than spread around. This research was especially persuasive since it was not a laboratory-based study but one which examined performance on a wide variety of military tasks over a two-month period. The findings suggested that groups composed of high ability people performed better than would have been predicted by the sum of their abilities.

A number of models of personality in teams have been proposed in the psychological literature. For example many organizations have tried to achieve compatibility within teams in the cognitive styles of members, by using the Myers-Briggs Type Indicator assessment instrument (a questionnaire measure of cognitive style). However, there is little research evidence presently available showing a relationship between compatibility and team performance.

Another popular approach is Belbin's Team Roles Model. Belbin argues that there are nine 'team personality' types (see below) which people display and that it is important to achieve a balance of these team personality types within a team. He argues that a mix of the nine team role types is required for a team to perform effectively. Individuals themselves will usually have a mix of team role types in their personality profiles and so, within teams of only three or four individuals there may, nevertheless, be primary and secondary team role types which cover the nine areas of team role functioning.

BELBIN'S TEAM ROLE THEORY

Based on research with over 200 teams conducting management business games at the Administrative Staff College, Henley, in the UK, Belbin identified nine team types. Almost always people have a mix of roles and will have dominant and sub-dominant roles.

Co-ordinator
The co-ordinator is a person-oriented leader. This person is trusting, accepting, dominant and is committed to team goals and objectives. The co-ordinator is a positive thinker who approves of goal attainment, struggle and effort in others. The co-ordinator is 'someone tolerant enough always to listen to others, but strong enough to reject their advice'. The co-ordinator may not stand out in a team and usually does not have a sharp intellect.

Shaper
The shaper is a task-focused leader, who abounds in nervous energy, who has high motivation to achieve and for whom winning is the name of the game. The shaper is committed to achieving ends and will 'shape' others into achieving the aims of the team. He or she will challenge, argue or disagree and will display aggression in the pursuit of goal achievement. Two or three shapers in a group, according to Belbin, can lead to conflict, aggravation and in-fighting.

Plant
The plant is a specialist idea maker characterized by high IQ and introversion while also being dominant and original. The plant tends to take radical approaches to team functioning and problems. Plants are more concerned with major issues than with details. Weaknesses are a tendency to disregard practical details and argumentativeness.

continued

continued—————————————————————————————

Resource investigator

'The resource investigator is the executive who is never in his room, and if he is, he is on the telephone'. The resource investigator is someone who explores opportunities and develops contacts. Resource investigators are good negotiators who probe others for information and support and pick up other people's ideas and develop them. They are characterized by sociability and enthusiasm and are good at liaison work and exploring resources outside the group. Weaknesses are a tendency to lose interest after initial fascination with an idea, and they are not usually a source of original ideas.

Company worker/implementer

Implementers are aware of external obligations and are disciplined, conscientious and have a good self-image. They tend to be tough-minded and practical, trusting and tolerant, respecting established traditions. They are characterized by low anxiety and tend to work for the team in a practical, realistic way. Implementers figure prominently in positions of responsibility in larger organizations. They tend to do the jobs that others do not want to do and do them well: for example, disciplining employees. Implementers are conservative, inflexible and slow to respond to new possibilities.

Monitor evaluator

According to the model, this is a judicious, prudent, intelligent person with a low need to achieve. Monitor evaluators contribute particularly at times of crucial decision making because they are capable of evaluating competing proposals. The monitor evaluator is not deflected by emotional arguments, is serious-minded, tends to be slow in coming to a decision because of a need to think things over and takes pride in never being wrong. Weaknesses are that they may appear dry and boring or even over-critical. They are not good at inspiring others. Those in high level appointments are often monitor evaluators.

Team worker

Team workers make helpful interventions to avert potential friction and enable difficult characters within the team to use their skills to positive ends. They tend to keep team spirit up and allow other members to contribute effectively. Their

—————————————————————————— -continued

continued –

diplomatic skills together with their sense of humour are assets to a team. They tend to have skills in listening, coping with awkward people and to be sociable, sensitive and people-oriented. They tend to be indecisive in moments of crisis and reluctant to do things that might hurt others.

Completer finishers

The completer finisher, dots the 'i's and crosses the 't's. He or she gives attention to detail, aims to complete and to do so thoroughly. They make steady effort and are consistent in their work. They are not so interested in the glamour of spectacular success. Weaknesses, according to Belbin, are that they tend to be over anxious and have difficulty letting go and delegating work.

Specialist

The specialist provides knowledge and technical skills which are in rare supply within the team. They are often highly introverted and anxious and tend to be self-starting, dedicated and committed. Their weaknesses are single-mindedness and a lack of interest in other peoples' subjects.

The effectiveness of teams is dependent upon a number of psychological factors which can inhibit or improve performance.

□ Subtle processes such as social loafing, hierarchical effects, and personality differences can dramatically inhibit team performance.

□ Within organizational settings, teams are usually put together and allowed to function without attempts being made to ensure effective functioning.

□ The most important elements of team management are linking individual and team goals and the design of the team task.

□ At the same time there must be regular clear and accurate feedback to the team on its performance over time in order to promote team effectiveness.

Overall, it should be clear from the topics covered in this chapter that team performance is far more complex than might be assumed. Therefore, practical guidelines based on scientific and applied understanding of team processes need to be offered to ensure optimum team functioning.

Chapter Two

Team Vision

'Whatever you can do, or dream you can, begin it.
Boldness has genius, power and magic in it. Begin it now'.

(Goethe).

DEFINING TEAM VISION

The overriding reason why people work in teams is because they
share a common goal or purpose which they believe will be
achieved more successfully if they work together than if they work
individually. This notion of shared purpose or shared vision is the
defining element of teams at work. By taking the time to clearly
define team vision, purpose and objectives, those who work within
teams have a greater chance of being effective and creative in their
work.

Confusion surrounds the use of words such as 'vision', 'mission
statement', 'objectives' and 'goals'. A useful way of thinking about
the meaning of these notions is to see them as parts of a tree. (See
the diagram on page 16.) Vision represents the base of the tree
growing from its roots in the values, skills and beliefs of those
within the team. The mission statement or trunk is the observable
statement of the team's purpose. The team objectives are then the
main branches of the tree which produce the goals (the twigs).
Finally, the action plans for achieving goals can be seen as the
leaves or foliage giving the tree its colour.

An example will illustrate the difference between the concepts.
Consider the vision of the Springwood Primary Health Care Team:

Team Vision: Springwood Primary Health Care Team
❏ *To give patients responsibility for their health and to make health
promotion our primary orientation rather than illness treatment. We are*

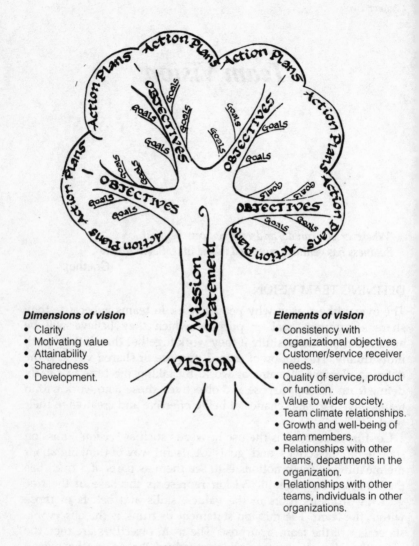

Dimensions of vision
- Clarity
- Motivating value
- Attainability
- Sharedness
- Development.

Elements of vision
- Consistency with organizational objectives
- Customer/service receiver needs.
- Quality of service, product or function.
- Value to wider society.
- Team climate relationships.
- Growth and well-being of team members.
- Relationships with other teams, departments in the organization.
- Relationships with other teams, individuals in other organizations.

VALUES, SKILLS, BELIEFS
OF
TEAM MEMBERS

Figure 2: From values to vision to action plans

*also committed to collaborative working together with patients, each other
and the community. We place great emphasis on holistic approaches to
health and the growth and well-being of our patients. We have a
fundamental commitment to excellence in primary health care with the
aim of improving the quality of life for the whole community. This vision
is based on our shared values of:*

- *respect for other human beings,*
- *cooperation to achieve shared goals,*
- *the importance of freedom of choice for all individuals,*
- *the importance of equality of treatment and opportunity for all within
  our primary health care catchment area,*
- *commitment to effectiveness and excellence in our work, with the
  overall aim of improving the quality of life of our patients, those in the
  community and of all those who work in this practice.*

This vision of the primary health care team sets out the principal
values which underlie and drive the work of the team. It also indicates the degree of cohesion between the various aspects of the
vision statement and represents an ideal for which to aim.

The mission statement of the team
❏ *'Our mission is to promote the health, growth and well-being of all of
those in our community, including patients, relatives, community
members and practice members by respecting the individual, encouraging
co-operation and collaboration and emphasizing excellence in all we do.'*

This mission statement provides a short motivating set of words,
summarizing and encapsulating the principal elements of the
team's vision. It serves as a daily reminder to those who work in or
with the team of the kinds of orientations that are expected in their
joint working. It is a motivating symbol, helping the team to
achieve its overall aims, and to make important choices at times
when there is uncertainty about a decision. It provides a clear
pointer to the directions the team should take when presented with
alternative ways forward, or when presented with difficult decisions about the team's work.

Team objectives
❏ *Springwood defined the following objectives as a result of articulating
its vision statement:*
1. *Increase the participation of patients in all aspects of the Springwood
   primary health care practice.*
2. *Emphasise health promotion as much as illness treatment in work with
   patients.*

3. *Involve all those who work in the practice in setting goals and in decision-making.*
4. *Promote the growth and well-being of practice members.*
5. *Improve health care in the Springwood community.*
6. *Aim for excellence in all of our practice activities.*
7. *Develop greater knowledge of holistic and alternative approaches to health care in the community.*

These objectives are derived directly from the vision of the team and from its mission statement. They describe clearly the overall aims that team members have for the practice's work.

In order to illustrate the goals of the practice and how they are derived from objectives, consider the goals relating to objective 3:

Example: Objective 3 (above)
❑ *To involve all those who work in the practice in setting goals and in decision-making.*

Goals to encourage group participation
1. *To encourage receptionists, district nurses, health visitors, practice nurses, practice manager and other staff to participate in staff meetings.*
2. *To encourage all staff members to input their views on the goals of the practice.*
3. *To encourage all staff to share information with one another so that they have sufficient knowledge of practice activities to influence practice goals.*
4. *To encourage all staff to interact regularly in order to encourage joint influence over the activities of the practice.*
5. *To encourage all staff members to make their views known in order that they can have some influence over decisions which are made in the team.*

These goals can then be translated directly into the leaves of the tree as action plans. Action plans constitute specific actions to be taken in order to achieve the goals which will help towards the achievement of objectives. For example, in relation to the goal 1 (above) of encouraging all of those involved in the practice to take part in meetings, Springwood created the following action plan:

Action plan
❑ **Objective 3, goal 1 (as above)**
1. *Weekly meetings will be held every Tuesday afternoon from 2.30pm–4.00pm prior to the afternoon surgery. All staff are encouraged to attend. The agenda for the meeting and notification of the meeting will be circulated by the practice manager 24 hours beforehand.*

2. *These meetings will be chaired, but the Chair will rotate in alphabetical order around all of those in the practice team who wish to contribute by taking the role of Chair. The person will chair the meeting for a period of six calendar months.*
3. *Every six months the practice manager will set up a full one-day meeting where the team reviews its objectives, strategies and processes at a congenial location, to be chaired by a facilitator from the Family Health Services Authority. All members of staff are encouraged to attend this meeting and to make their views known about the practice's work. On this day, locums will be appointed to ensure that the practice's work is covered.*

From the vision grows a solid mission statement from which can be derived the principal objectives of the team. These guide the development of more detailed goals, which translate into action plans. In turn they should prompt specific actions by team members. Articulating the vision provides the basis for all of the team's activities. Surprisingly, few teams take the time to work out their vision, mission statement, objectives, goals and action plans.

➤ *Vision is a shared idea of a valued outcome which provides the motivation for the team's work.*

In order to develop a statement of team vision, a number of dimensions must be considered. These should include its clarity, motivating value, attainability, the extent to which it is shared by team members, and its ongoing development. Each of these dimensions is described below.

THE DIMENSIONS OF TEAM VISION

CLARITY
In order for a team to determine its objectives, goals and actions it must have a clear vision. If team members are unsure of what the shared orientations, values and purposes of their colleagues are, it is difficult for them to articulate a clear statement which encapsulates these orientations and values. This requires that team members communicate about their work values and orientations. They must then find a form of words which expresses accurately and clearly these shared values, interests and motivations. Later in this chapter the steps in fashioning a clear statement of vision are described.

MOTIVATING VALUE

The values that we bring to our work influence the effort we put into it. Consequently for a team to work well together, team members must have some shared sense of the value of their work. For example, in health care settings people do work which accords with a basic value of helping others. To the extent that the vision reflects the underlying values of the team it is likely to motivate team loyalty, effort and commitment.

In other settings it may not be so easy to engage people's values in the organizational objectives of the team. However, values about excellence in work, respect for individuals, and the growth and well-being of team members can be expressed within almost any context. For example, a team engaged in collecting financial debts may value treating all individuals with respect and consideration. It may also decide that team member skills should be enhanced and developed in order to encourage greater excellence both in team working and in relationships with others. Working in teams, where the vision or values are inconsistent with one's own, can create difficulties. For example, within a team in a personnel department which is being directed to appoint people on contracts offering little job security, poor pay, and poor career development opportunities, team members may work less hard simply because the approach is inconsistent with their values. Many people experience working in situations where they feel that the work that they are required to do is in conflict with their core values. The consequence is that we work less hard or look for alternative jobs – we are less motivated and less committed.

ATTAINABILITY

'That man is truly free who desires what he is able to perform, and does what he desires'.

(Rousseau)

When a team is set unattainable goals it can have a de-motivating effect. It may also lead to some of the problems described in the last chapter, such as free riding and social loafing. For example, a research and development team may be given the task of producing a new method of telephone communication such that callers who receive an engaged signal when they telephone have the option of holding until the other party's call is complete and then the phone automatically rings out. However, the space of time within which the team is required to achieve this system may be so short (for example, three months) that they have no realistic chance of achieving the goal in the required time. Consequently their commitment and motivation may be substantially reduced. This depends to some extent upon the nature of the task they are being asked to perform. A top management team at OXFAM may be less de-motivated by the difficulty of achieving food for all by the year 2000, simply because of the enormous motivating value of the vision of the team. There is, therefore, a trade-off between attainability and the motivating value of a team's vision.

SHAREDNESS

In all of the work that my colleagues and I have conducted with management teams, primary health care teams, social services teams, oil company teams etc, we have found that one aspect of vision is particularly important in predicting effectiveness – the extent to which the vision is shared – which is itself dependent upon the extent to which the vision is negotiated. In many organizations top management prescribe the vision and objectives of teams. This is self-contradictory: *a team cannot be prescribed a vision; it must develop its own.* When top management define a team's vision and objectives, the team is less motivated and effective than when the team defines its own. Where team members feel they have made a real contribution to the determination of the team's vision and objectives, they are likely to work hard to co-operate and achieve their shared, valued outcomes.

ABILITY TO DEVELOP

A danger of team working is that decisions about vision made at one point in time, become cast in stone. Because teams are constantly evolving – the people within the teams are changing their views, developing new skills and changing values – it is important that the vision of the team evolves in the same way. Similarly, the environment within which the team operates goes through change; organizations change strategies and society changes its views. Currently, for example, there is much emphasis upon environmental protection and equal opportunities. Teams which formerly might not have considered these issues may now need to give them careful consideration. Consequently a team's vision must be regularly reviewed in order to ensure that it is alive, evolving, up-to-date and representative of the changing values and orientations of team members. Otherwise, team vision can become a strait jacket within which the team is prevented from developing in new directions.

THE ELEMENTS OF TEAM VISION

It is possible to consider eight major elements of team vision which are the areas upon which a team's vision may focus:

1. CONSISTENCY WITH ORGANIZATIONAL OBJECTIVES

In some circumstances a team may decide that it is important for its own values, purposes and orientations to act as a minority group which aims to bring about change in organizational objectives. For example, within the UK National Health Service there has been considerable debate about the conflict which exists between providing health care and reducing spending. Some teams have attempted to subvert the second orientation where they see it as conflicting with their aim of providing quality health care for all, regardless of priorities determined by a Regional Health Authority. So, in some circumstances, a team may work effectively when its vision contradicts stated organizational objectives. However, it is very important that teams are clear about when they wish to act as minority groups in order that they may develop appropriate strategies to bring about the kinds of organizational change they wish. This is an issue discussed in more depth in Chapter 9.

2. CUSTOMER/SERVICE RECEIVER NEEDS

To what extent will the team work to provide excellence in service to its customers, whether they be customers within or outside the organization? To what extent are service receivers seen as people who are to be merely satisfied, rather than people who are to receive the best quality of service available? For example, a teaching team in a university department might prefer to emphasize research excellence above the quality of teaching provided to students. Alternatively, they may strive to admit as many students as possible, putting pedagogical excellence second. A car maintenance team may emphasise satisfying the customer above ever-increasing profitability (though these two may not necessarily contradict one another).

3. QUALITY OF PRODUCT, SERVICE OR FUNCTION

A major emphasis within organizations in the 1990s is the quality of services and functioning within organizational settings. Team members may also discuss the extent to which top quality will characterize their own working relationships. This may be reflected in the speed with which requests for information within the team are met, and also the quality of information which is eventually produced.

4. VALUE TO WIDER SOCIETY

It is unusual for teams to take time out to consider the value of their work for the wider society. Consideration of this and ways in which it can be enhanced is an important way of encouraging both team cohesion and greater team effectiveness. Such consideration may promote conflict if team members perceive their work to be irrelevant to the wider society or if there are conflicts between team members about the potential value of the team's work. However, throughout this book it is argued that such conflict enables team members to achieve clear perception of the purposes of their work and therefore enhances team effectiveness and creativity.

5. TEAM CLIMATE RELATIONSHIPS

Team climate relationships are often neglected when teams discuss their functioning. If team members have such difficult relationships that members are inclined to leave the team, long term team viability is threatened. Teams therefore need to consider the type of team climate they wish to create. Team climate refers to aspects of teamwork such as warmth, humour, amount of conflict, mutual support, sharing, backbiting, emphasis of status, participation, information sharing, level of criticism of each other's work, and support for new ideas. Chapters 3 to 8 consider various ways in which the team climate can be enhanced.

6. GROWTH AND WELL-BEING OF TEAM MEMBERS

Another element of vision is support for the skill development and well-being of team members. Growth, skill development and challenge are central elements of work life and teams can be a major source of support. They may provide opportunities for skill sharing and support for new training. One issue is the extent to which team members will support skill development and training which may further someone's career, although this may not contribute immediately to team effectiveness.

Another area of concern for a team is the general well-being of its members. This is especially true for those working in conditions of high stress, such as caring professionals. The social support which team members provide can have a buffering effect, preventing stress-related illnesses.

7. RELATIONSHIPS WITH OTHER TEAMS AND DEPARTMENTS IN THE ORGANIZATION

Teams rarely operate in isolation. They interact with other teams and departments within the organization, for example, in co-operating in cross-functional teams or competing for scarce resources. Therefore teams need to decide what orientation – co-operation or competition – they will adopt towards other teams and departments within their organization.

Groups often compete as a result of 'group identification', where people tend to favour their own group and discriminate against other groups, leading to destructive working relationships. For example, health visitors working in community health settings may find themselves in conflict with GPs or with district nurses. Equally, they may find themselves co-operating closely and working effectively with other professionals. Those groups which are most successful seem to have thought through very carefully what kind of relationships they wish to have in order to achieve their overall goals.

8. RELATIONSHIPS WITH TEAMS OUTSIDE THE ORGANIZATION

Similar issues arise in considering team relationships with other organizations. For example, BBC TV Continuing Education production teams are concerned with issues which affect the whole community. In producing programmes about how families can function most effectively, they may therefore want to work closely with the relevant voluntary and professional organizations. On the other hand, a team may decide to take a very critical orientation to the work of these organizations and may wish to distance itself in the making of a programme. In order for a team to have a clear shared vision about its work, it must make explicit (where relevant) the quality and nature of relationships it seeks with organizations and individuals.

This chapter began by emphasizing the fundamental importance of team vision for effective team working. This is because without a clear beacon to guide it the team can often be diverted from its course by organizational demands, the changing interests of team members, or other external pressures. With a clear sense of vision, rooted in the shared values of members, the team will maintain a good course towards its valued aims and objectives.

Chapter Three

Being Part of a Team

Being part of a team means being responsible for team objectives, team strategies and team processes. While team work implies differentiation of roles and responsibilities and thereby that people will take leadership positions, this does not mean that the team leader is solely responsible for determining team objectives, strategies, processes and outcomes. On the contrary, in effective work teams, all team members are aware of and sensitive to team functioning.

THE ELEMENTS OF TEAM PARTICIPATION

Being part of a team involves participation. Toby Wall, a colleague of mine, suggests there are three fundamental elements to participation. These are the three I's of: Interaction, Information sharing and Influence over decision-making.

1. INTERACTION
In order for a group of individuals who share a common goal to be called a team they must have some minimal ongoing interaction, otherwise their efforts are essentially uncoordinated and unaggregated. Teams interact during task performance and socially; both are equally important. Social interactions might include parties, lunches or informal chats in the corridors to discuss family matters or sporting events. These interactions strengthen the social bonding, cohesion and familiarity which enable people to feel safe with one another. Interaction during task performance provides an exchange of information, communication etc, which enables the team to co-ordinate individual member efforts to achieve their shared goals.

Case study: team interaction

❑ *I was once asked to act as a facilitator for a team which provided consultancy services to a large organization. On the first day the team emphasized how effective they were as a team. However, after an hour or two of interaction the team had split into two opposing groups in separate rooms, accompanied by strong expressions of anger and hostility. It emerged that the team had not met together for over 18 months and had assumed they shared similar orientations and objectives in their work. In fact, team members were working at cross purposes and, even after two days together, there was still some tension over their differing orientations to the work. This seemed to be due to the surprise of discovering these differences rather than to any intrinsic incompatibility in their work orientations.*

What this case suggests is that interaction is an important part of team functioning. Without regular meetings, both formal and informal, important information is not exchanged and assumptions and expectations may be built up which are not matched by reality. Team members may begin to diverge in their views about what is important for the team, and perceptions of other team members' actions may be incorrect. Misapprehension and misunderstanding can lead to conflict and lack of co-ordination in terms of task processes. These in turn lead to lowered team effectiveness.

It is not possible to specify any ideal frequency of interaction. Some teams will need to meet more often than others and meetings between some team members will need to be more frequent than between other team members. However, teams should meet minimally once a month, in order to update one another on developments. Every six months too, it is valuable for teams to take time out to reflect upon and modify as necessary their objectives, their strategies for achieving those objectives and team processes such as communication and participation in decision-making.

2. INFORMATION SHARING

Information in a team context is data which alters the understanding of the team as a whole and/or of individual team members. Monitoring information sharing is essential for team effectiveness.

Information can be rich or poor to the extent that it alters understanding; i.e.the more it alters understanding the richer it is. For example, in a changeover of nursing teams in a psychiatric ward, information relating to the potentially violent or suicidal behaviour of a patient i.e. how aggressive or unstable the patient has been during the course of the shift, is rich information. It communicates to the nurse taking over, the likelihood that the patient will assault another patient or a member of staff or commit a self-injurious act. On the other hand, a computer print-out of the number of visits to children under five years of age made by a health visitor during the course of one month may communicate relatively little information to their supervisor, since it provides no indication of the difficulty of the visits or the quality of the work.

The medium of transfer of information is determined by its richness. The least rich information is transferred by paper or electronic mail messages. Slightly richer information is given in the form of telephone conversations or video conferencing, but information is most richly transferred when people talk face-to-face. Voice inflexion, facial expression, body posture and gestures all add to the richness of information transfer. Moreover, in face-to-face meetings it is possible to ask questions and explore issues in depth.

INFORMATION SHARING IN THE TEAM

EXERCISE 3

What information do you currently receive from each team member?

Name of Team Member	Content of Information received	Current medium (Face to face, E-Mail)	Current frequency
1.			
2.			
3.			
4.			
5.			
6.			
7.			
8.			

What information would you like from each team member?

Name of Team Member	Content of Information received	Desired medium	Desired frequency
1.			
2.			
3.			
4.			
5.			
6.			
7.			
8.			

Within a team setting the ideal medium is face to face except for routine messages. However, there is a temptation to avoid such direct communication since this may take up time. In general, teams err on the side of electronic mail messages and communicate too little face to face. Yet the whole basis of team work is communication, co-ordination, co-operation and transfer of information in the richest possible form. Consequently there is a real need for team members to address issues about information sharing and communication and to examine the media that they use to transfer this information.

Case study: Manufacturing success
❏ *Information flows vary enormously, depending upon the organizational settings. On a visit to an innovative manufacturing company in Scotland, I met the Personnel Director who had previously worked in the Civil Service. He told me that it took him a year of working in the manufacturing company to receive the number of written memoranda that he normally received in a week within the Civil Service. Another change was a much higher level of face-to-face communication in the manufacturing company, which led to a much richer understanding. The company was characterized by enormous flexibility, few rules and regulations and a high degree of innovativeness.*

3. INFLUENCE OVER DECISION-MAKING
Traditionally, the notion of participation has been understood as the extent of influence over decision-making and it is to this topic that we now turn. Participation can involve simply superficial consultation where team members' views are sought but in practice the team leader or team managers make decisions based on their own judgement. At the other extreme is total democracy where all decisions are taken by a team vote; but this can lead to decision-making 'paralysis' rather than team effectiveness. In some primary health care teams, for example, attempts to increase all members' influence over decision-making have tended to fail since the teams have become less effective as a result.

There are many situations where teams need leaders. In moments of crisis there may not be time for the whole team to discuss the appropriate course of action in depth. One individual may be required to grasp the nettle and take decisions for the good of the whole team. In most circumstances, however, teams can sanction individuals to take the decisions in specific areas of the team's activity.

In order to achieve a balance between excessive democracy and authoritarianism, team reviews of decision-making processes should be conducted every six months to a year. The purpose of these reviews should be to determine which team members should take executive decisions on behalf of the team and in which areas.

GROUP DECISION-MAKING

A principal assumption behind the structuring of organizational functioning into work groups is that groups will make better decisions than individual group members working alone. However, a good deal of research has shown that groups are subject to social processes which undermine their decision-making effectiveness. While work groups tend to make decisions which are better than the average of decisions made by individual members, they consistently fall short of the quality of decisions made by the best individual member. The implications of this for the functioning of boards and senior executive teams are considerable. Organizational behaviourists and social psychologists have therefore devoted considerable effort to identifying the social processes which create deficiencies in group decision-making:

1. **Personality factors** can affect social behaviour in various ways. For example, any shyness by individual members, who may be hesitant to offer their opinions and knowledge assertively, will mean that they fail to contribute fully to the group's store of knowledge.

2. Group members are subject to **social conformity** effects causing them to withhold opinions and information contrary to the majority view – especially an organizationally-dominant view.

3. Group members may lack **communication skills** and so be unable to present their views and knowledge successfully. The person who has mastered impression management within the organization may disproportionately influence group decisions even in the absence of expertise.

4. The group may be dominated by particular individuals who take up disproportionate '**air time**' or argue so vigorously with the opinion of others that their own views prevail. It is noteworthy that 'air time' and expertise are correlated in high-performing groups and uncorrelated in groups that perform poorly.

5. Particular group members may be **egocentric** (such as senior organizational members whose egocentricity may have carried them to the top) and consequently unwilling to consider opinions or knowledge offered by other group members contrary to their own.

6. **Status and hierarchy** effects can cause some members' contributions to be valued and attended to disproportionately. When a senior executive is present in a meeting, his or her views are likely to have an undue influence on the outcome.

7. **'Risky shift'** refers to the tendency of work groups to make more extreme decisions than the average of individual members' opinions or decisions. Group decisions tend to be either more risky or more conservative than the average of individuals members' opinions or decisions. Thus shifts in the extremity of decisions affecting the competitive strategy of an organization can occur simply as a result of group processes rather than for rational or well-judged reasons.

8. In his study of failures in policy decisions, social psychologist Irving Janis, identified the phenomenon of **'groupthink'**, whereby tightly-knit groups may err in their decision-making because they are more concerned with achieving agreement than with the quality of the decisions made. This can be especially threatening to organizational functioning where different departments see themselves as competing with one another, promoting 'in-group' favouritism and groupthink.

9. The **social loafing effect** is the tendency of individuals in group situations to work less hard than they do when individual contributions can be identified and evaluated. In organizations, individuals may put less effort into achieving quality decisions in meetings, if they perceive that their contribution is hidden in overall group performance.

10. Diffusion of **responsibility** can inhibit individuals from taking responsibility for action when in the presence of others. People seem to assume that responsibility will be shouldered by others who are present in a situation requiring action. In organizational settings, individuals may fail to act in a crisis involving the functioning of expensive technology, assuming that others in their team are taking the responsibility for taking the necessary decisions. Consequently, the overall quality of group decisions is threatened.

11. The study of brainstorming groups shows that quantity and often quality of ideas produced by individuals working separately are consistently superior to those produced by a group working together. This is due to a '**production-blocking**' effect. Individuals are inhibited from both thinking of new ideas and offering them aloud to the group by the competing verbalizations of others.

THE STEP-LADDER TECHNIQUE FOR DECISION-MAKING

In order to overcome the problems of group decision-making described above, Rogelberg and colleagues have proposed a strategy called 'the step-ladder technique'. This has four require-ments:

1. Each group member must be given time to think through the particular problem or issue before entering the group and presenting his or her views.

2. As they enter the group, each member must present his or her preliminary views about the appropriate course of action before hearing the core group's preliminary solutions.

3. With the entry of each additional member to the core group, sufficient time to discuss the problem and proffer solutions is necessary.

4. A final decision must be delayed until all members of the group have had an opportunity to present their views.

The step-ladder technique involves giving each individual member of the team quiet time to reflect upon the particular problem in order to prepare his or her case, independent of other group members. It also gives time for each group member to present his or her views and for some discussion to take place after each presentation. Finally, decision-making is postponed until all group members have presented their views.

This approach to decision-making facilitates communication since all members of the group have an opportunity to present their views. This communication may lead to a greater number or range of ideas being presented since conformity processes will be minimized. It also inhibits social loafing effects since in-dividual accountability is emphasized and there is no opportunity for individual members to hide behind others' contributions.

Furthermore, because each member is required to present his or her views without the benefit of having heard all the other team members' views, disagreements are more likely and therefore the quality of decision-making and discussion may be improved. The group is exposed to the continual input of fresh ideas which have not been affected by group norms, and this may lead to a vigorous evaluation and exploration of contrasting ideas. Considerable evidence indicates that such exploration of divergent opinions within teams leads to better quality decision-making.

Another cause of poor decision-making is the tendency to go with the first acceptable solution rather than to generate a range of solutions and then to select the best option. By delaying decision-making until every group member has had an opportunity to present his or her views, the number of possible solutions or options available to the group is maximized.

A major deficiency of group decision-making is the failure of teams to out-perform their best individual member. Because the step-ladder technique increases the likelihood of each individual member being heard, opportunities for the best individual member to display his or her expertise are increased considerably. This is important because recent research has shown that unless the best individual member happens to be assertive and dominant, he or she is unlikely to influence group ratings. Where expertise and 'air time' are correlated, groups tend to perform well. In poor performing groups 'air time' and expertise tend to be uncorrelated.

How effective is the step-ladder technique? Research evidence indicates that there is no difference in the time taken for decision-making between groups using the step-ladder technique and conventional techniques. However, the quality of group decisions is generally significantly better than in conventional groups. Moreover, more than half the step-ladder groups exceed their best members' scores, compared with only one tenth of conventional groups.

These statistical findings tell one story, but the impressions of those in step-ladder groups reveal further important information. Step-ladder group members report feeling much less pressured to conform; tend to agree on the final group decision, perceive themselves as working unusually well together, and perceive the group as more friendly. They also see themselves as having worked harder on the task than do conventional group members. Moreover, there tends to be more questioning of views and ideas in step-ladder groups than in conventional groups.

In effect, step-ladder groups continually re-make their decisions, which has beneficial effects on group output. Interestingly, the most expert members in step-ladder groups report that they have more chance to say what they want (more so than any other group members), which suggests that the step-ladder approach reveals knowledge and individual expertise to other group members. In other words, better ideas are not only more likely to be expressed, but are more likely to be attended to and recognized as better.

A SHORT FORM OF THE STEP-LADDER TECHNIQUE

EXERCISE 4

1. Allow 10 minutes – all individuals within the group engage in analysing the problem and coming up with potential problem solutions.
2. Allow 10 minutes – group members work in pairs to present and discuss their respective solutions separate from other group members.
3. Allow 10 minutes – two pairs of individuals present their solutions to each other and discuss the solutions. This process continues until the whole group comes together.
4. The whole group considers solutions presented, final discussions take place and a decision is made. About 40–60 minutes should be allowed for creating the one best solution for the problem.

The step-ladder technique is a method of decision-making which can overcome some of the problems of team decision-making. By enabling members to participate fully, commitment, intrinsic interest, creativity and the input of all members' abilities, knowledge and skills are increased.

SAFETY IN TEAMS

It is a truism of human behaviour that commitment and involvement are most likely to occur when people feel safe. Just as the child who has strong and secure bonding with his or her parents is more likely to explore their surroundings more extensively, so too are people in groups more likely to take risks in introducing new and improved ways of doing things if they feel they are unlikely to be attacked or denigrated by other group members. The child taken to the park by a parent will be more likely to leave the parent's side sooner and make longer forays into the park if they are securely bonded and attached to that parent. Where children have poor relationships with their parents, they are likely to hover anxiously close rather than explore their new surroundings. In therapy, clients are likely to explore threatening aspects of their own experience when they feel supported and safe from attack by their therapist. It is not for purely ideological reasons that Carl Rogers urged therapists to adopt an attitude of unconditional positive regard for patients. Such an orientation is likely to induce feelings of safety and thereby encourage greater exploration of difficult experiences.

Similarly in team settings, it is important that team members perceive a climate of interpersonal safety, free from the possibility of attack or threat. Where the team is perceived as unsafe, members behave cautiously and maintain a kind of anxious watchfulness in their work. For example, if a practice nurse feels he or she is being criticized constantly by the general practitioners, they will be less likely to suggest new ways of doing things and offer ideas for improving team functioning. The nurses will also be less likely to exercise their own initiative in improving the quality of health care supplied by the team to the community. Each team member has a responsibility to promote safety. This involves encouraging others to offer their views and then supportively exploring those ideas.

Safety is the affective context within which people are more likely to engage in effective team working based on trust, acceptance, humour, warmth and support. Together these lead to the involvement, commitment and creativity of team members in team functioning and equally important, to a positive climate which enhances the mental health of people at work.

The next chapter examines what can go wrong in a team even when there are clear visions and objectives, and high levels of participation.

Chapter Four

Aiming for Excellence in Team Work

'Have you learned lessons only of those who admired you, and were tender with you and stood aside for you? Have you not learned great lessons from those who braced themselves against you, and disputed the passage with you?'

(Walt Whitman)

So far we have considered the importance of a clear vision or set of objectives along with high levels of participation in a team. However, these two elements are necessary but insufficient to guarantee effective team working. There is evidence that these very factors in isolation can be the seeds of disastrous outcomes.

Consider the following account as an illustration of how clear objectives and high levels of participation and cohesion may lead to quite the opposite in the effectiveness of team work. In 1961, the United States presidency was surrounded by an aura of optimism, enthusiam and vigour. President Kennedy and his advisors were young, enthusiastic and had captured the optimism of many Americans with their commitment to civil rights and democracy. However, at the beginning of the presidency, this group charac-terized by high levels of vision, cohesiveness and participation was responsible for one of the major foreign policy fiascos of the decade. This was the support of the invasion of Cuba in what became known as the Bay of Pigs affair. Against much intelligence information which indicated the likely failure of such an adventure, Kennedy and his advisors authorized the CIA to support Cuban exiles in an invasion. The invasion was easily repulsed and the exiles were taken prisoner or killed. Afterwards many commen-tators questioned how Kennedy and his advisors could have come to the conclusion that the adventure would have been successful.

GROUPTHINK

In a revealing analysis of the affair, Irving Janis (1972) came to the conclusion that a dangerous pattern of group processes was responsible. Janis argued that Kennedy's cabinet was prone to the detrimental effects of 'groupthink'. Groupthink arises where five conditions are present:

1. The team is a highly cohesive group of individuals who are more concerned with their own cohesiveness and unanimity than with quality of decision making.

2. The group typically insulates itself from information and opinions from outside and particularly those which go against the group view.

3. Members of the group rarely engage in any kind of systematic search through the available options for appropriate solutions, choosing instead to go with the first available option on which there is a consensus.

4. The group is under pressure to achieve a decision.

5. The group is dominated by one strong individual.

Groupthink can be diagnosed by the presence of one or more of the following tendencies:

- Where the conditions for groupthink exist, a cohesive group will exert strong pressures on dissenting individuals to conform to the view of the majority.

- The group is characterized by a shared illusion of unanimity and correctness. Dean Rusk who was Kennedy's Secretary of State for Defence described how there was a 'curious atmosphere of assumed consensus' within the group.

- Members of the group ignore or dismiss cues that there may be dissent within the group. Indeed some members of the Kennedy cabinet later described how they had felt inhibited from offering ideas or views opposing the Bay of Pigs plan, even when they felt privately that there were major problems with it.

- Group members actively prevent information from outside the group being admitted to the group's discussion. Bobby Kennedy (US Attorney General at the time), described how he had become a self-appointed 'mind guard' to the group whereby he had threatened outsiders holding adverse opinions with accusations of disloyalty to the President.

- Where strong Groupthink pressures exist, outgroups are ridiculed as 'too stupid' to be a threat or 'too untrustworthy' to be negotiated with. *'The picture ... therefore, is of a tightly knit group, isolated from outside influences, converging rapidly on to a normatively 'correct' point of view and thereafter being convinced of its own rectitude and the inferiority of all other competing opinions (or groups)'*. Brown (1988).

Groupthink consists of the following characteristics:
- An illusion of vulnerability;
- Excessive optimism and risk-taking;
- A tendency to rationalize and discount warnings;
- Stereotyping of the opposition;
- Self-censorship;
- Failure to use expert opinion plus selection bias.

All lead to a failure to solve problems effectively because of a need for unanimity and cohesiveness.

GROUP PRESSURES TO CONFORM

The effects of group pressures on individuals to conform have been well established. In Asch's research some participants were shown into a room to join others already there. Those in the room before the experimental participants were, unbeknown to the experimental participants, confederates of the researcher. A series of vertical lines was flashed on a screen and both participants and 'confederates' were asked to determine which of three lines was of the same size as a standard line, stimuli which were unambiguous. On most occasions people chose the line which equalled the length of the standard line but on a number of occasions they unanimously picked a wrong line. Fully three-quarters of the experimental participants went along with the majority on at least one occasion, even though subsequently they reported having been aware that this was the incorrect line. They indicated that this was due to a desire not to be different from the majority, especially where the majority was unanimous. Similar effects have been found in a number of other research studies over time. Majority influence effects have a powerful impact upon the behaviour of people in groups.

Encouragingly, there are individual differences in the extent to which people will go along with the majority. In Asch's experiments some individuals (25% of those who participated) never went along with the majority, while others conformed to the majority opinion on all occasions. Moreover, the size of the group is important in majority influence. The results showed that when an individual was confronted with only one person who was responding in an inconsistent manner, he or she was unlikely to be influenced. Under pressure from a majority of three, conformity jumped to 32%, from only 14% with a majority of two. If individuals were supported by another dissenting individual within a group then participants answered incorrectly in only 9% of cases compared with 36% when they were in a minority of one.

OBEDIENCE TO AUTHORITY

In hierarchical groups, there is a tendency for people to be obedient to authority. Within a group situation where there is a dominant leader, people may well be inclined to go along with the leader rather than to assert their own opinions. In a chilling demonstration of this danger, Stanley Milgram examined the extent to which individuals would be obedient to the commands of an experimenter to give electric shocks to an individual learning word-pairs. The person learning the word-pairs was, in fact, a confederate of the experimenter and the electric shocks were faked. Out of 40 people participating in the experiment, 26 obeyed the orders of the experimenter to the end and continued to give (apparent) electric shock punishment to the learners, up to and beyond the point at which it was thought the learners had been severely injured. This was despite the fact that in many instances the individuals administering the shocks were clearly suffering great tension and concern about what they were doing. One observer related:

> I observed a mature and initially poised businessman enter the laboratory smiling and confident. Within 20 minutes he was reduced to a twitching, stuttering wreck who was rapidly approaching a point of nervous collapse. He constantly pulled on his ear lobe, and twisted his hand. At one point he pushed his fist into his forehead and muttered: 'Oh God, let's stop it'.

Yet he continued to listen to every word of the experimenter, and obeyed to the end. This research suggests that there are dangers in group settings which can result in conformity and obedience to authority in the face of clear rational evidence against a given course of action.

TEAM DEFENCE MECHANISMS

If we think of a team as somehow a 'living entity' in its own right, it would not be surprising for it to have developed mechanisms to survive in a changing environment. Just like an organism, a team develops an immune system to fight threats to its stability. Often this system is such an integral part of the norms and unwritten rules of the team that it is very difficult to detect. Such team defences are sometimes referred to as 'defensive routines' which are set into motion automatically and without deliberate intention on the part of any individual. At their best, these defensive routines help protect the team from experiencing unnecessary turmoil. They are, however, designed to reduce pain and embarrassment, and in doing so can inhibit team functioning. Moreover, in trying to maintain the status quo, team members may employ defensive routines which prevent the team from dealing with the root causes of problems. The nature of team defensive routines is such that they are often undiscussable and their undiscussability is also undiscussable!

Defensive routines are used to make the unreasonable seem reasonable, and are often employed in the name of caring and diplomacy. One example of a defensive routine is where team members continually blame the organization, senior managers and resources problems for difficulties that the team is experiencing. So regardless of what goes on within the team, problems are always perceived to be based on what is occurring outside. Consequently, a kind of cohesion is maintained between people within the team who collude together in not addressing their own performance problems.

A COMMITMENT TO EXCELLENCE AND TASK ORIENTATION

How can a team function in ways which minimize conformity, obedience to authority and the effects of defensive routines? Structures, strategies, techniques and norms can all be developed which enable teams to resist these influences effectively. One technique described earlier is the step-ladder technique of decision-making (see chapter 3). Team structure can also be changed to reduce hierarchies within the team.

What other methods can be used? Below, some of the techniques or orientations for ensuring the highest quality of group performance and decision-making are considered.

TASK ORIENTATION / CONSTRUCTIVE CONTROVERSY

Task orientation refers to a group's critical orientation towards its own performance, or more specifically, group members' preparedness to examine their team performance critically. Dean Tjosvold of Simon Fraser University in Canada has coined the term 'constructive controversy' to describe the conditions necessary for effective questioning within a group.

Research evidence amassed by Tjosvold and others, suggests that when groups explore opposing opinions carefully and discuss them in a co-operative context, quality of decision-making and group effectiveness is dramatically increased.

'Controversy when discussed in a co-operative context promotes elaboration of views, the search for new information and ideas and the integration of apparently opposing positions'.   (Tjosvold, 1991)

Tjosvold believes that a lack of constructive controversy can lead to decisions such as the Bay of Pigs invasion and the Challenger space shuttle disaster. In the latter case, it was suggested that engineers suppressed information that opinions differed about the appropriateness of flying the shuttle in cold weather.

Tjosvold argues that there are three elements to controversy: elaborating positions, searching for understanding and integrating perspectives.

1. First, team members should carefully describe their positions, explaining how they have come to their decisions in relation to any particular issue within the team. They should also indicate to what extent they are confident or uncertain about the positions they have adopted.

2. People with opposing viewpoints should seek out more information about others' positions and attempt to restate them as clearly as possible. There should be attempts to explore areas of common ground in opposing positions along with an emphasis

on personal regard for individuals whose positions oppose their own. This process will lead to greater creativity and more productive outcomes.

3. Team members should encourage integration by working to resolve controversy based on the principle of excellence in decision-making. Attempts to influence team members towards a solution should be on the basis of shared, rational understanding rather than attempted dominance. Finally, members should strive for consensus by combining team ideas wherever possible rather than using techniques to reduce controversy, such as majority voting. Strategies such as voting may merely postpone controversy. Table 1 shows the conditions within which team constructive controversy can exist.

Table 1: Constructive Controversy

Constructive controversy is necessary for:
- Creativity
- Independent thinking
- Quality checking
- Professional development
- Team development.

Constructive controversy is characterized by:
- Exploration of opposing opinions
- Open-minded consideration and understanding
- Concern for integration of ideas
- Concern with high quality solutions
- Tolerance of diversity in the team.

Constructive controversy exists when there are:
- Co-operative team climates
- Shared team goals
- Personal competence confirmed
- Processes of mutual influence.

Constructive controversy does not exist when:
- There are competitive team climates
- Team goals are not primary
- Personal competence is questioned
- There are processes of attempted dominance.

DEVIL'S ADVOCACY

In order to cope with the potential flaws in his Cabinet's decision-making strategies President Kennedy introduced a number of initiatives. First he brought alternative and often extreme viewpoints into Cabinet discussions to promote diversity of opinion and more creative decision-making. Secondly, he promoted the idea of delaying decisions until they were necessary rather than rushing to first solutions. Thirdly, he appointed someone within the group to challenge quickly and vigorously any decisions considered by the group. Bobby Kennedy, the then Attorney General, was appointed to this position of devil's advocate. He later described how during the Cuban missile crisis in 1963, his role was to criticize and attack opinions offered within the group in order to ensure that arguments were carefully examined for strengths and weaknesses. This led, it is argued, to better quality decision-making.

The **Devil's Advocate** is the individual within the team whose responsibility it is to challenge arguments and ideas and seek out weaknesses within them. However, it is important that this role rotates, otherwise the process becomes identified with one individual and may be discounted by other team members. By appointing a rotating devil's advocate within the group opinions, ideas, suggestions and strategies are carefully scrutinized by at least one team member whose job it is to promote controversy and conflict in order to ensure excellence in functioning.

NEGATIVE BRAINSTORMING

Negative brainstorming is a particularly useful technique for promoting excellence and critical thinking in groups. It can be used for testing a new proposal, or for evaluating an existing strategy, practice or objective. The technique can be achieved in the following three stages:

Step 1. Once a promising idea has been proposed (or in the case of an existing practice, the practice or strategy has been clearly identified), the group brainstorms around all possible negative aspects or consequences of the idea. This brainstorming should be as uninhibited as positive brainstorming in the classical approach (see Chapter 1). The intention is to generate a list of all the possible negative aspects of the idea or strategy no matter how wild or fanciful these possibilities might appear.

Step 2. Team members choose four or five of the most salient criticisms, and examine these in more detail. At least one of these criticisms should be a wild or fanciful criticism.

Step 3. The group then considers how the idea or existing practice could be modified to deal with each of the criticisms in turn. This third stage of the process is, therefore, essentially constructive in that the group is seeking to build on a new or existing practice in order to counter the major criticisms of it.

It may be that some fundamental weakness or difficulty is identified, which the group sees no way of overcoming. In this case, the idea or the existing practice may be abandoned. However, this is a benefit rather than a disadvantage of the process since it enables groups to identify at an early stage, any idea or approach which is likely to be unsuccessful.

This exercise is useful when an idea has reached the adoption and implementation phase of decision-making. In addition to drawing out the weak points of an idea before it is implemented, it also encourages constructive criticism. People are sometimes inhibited in their criticisms for fear of causing offence. This approach makes it clear that criticism is directed at ideas and practices rather than people. If it is used on a regular basis 'criticizing ideas as a way of improving on them' becomes accepted by the group as good practice.

STAKE-HOLDER ANALYSIS

This is a useful method for exploring an issue in more depth and improving upon existing and proposed solutions. It is based on the idea that people are much less resistant to changes, as long as careful and creative thought has been put into considering how those changes will affect them in practice. Stake-holders are all those interested individuals and groups, both internal and external to the team, who affect or who are affected by the team's objectives and practices.

The technique involves the team, or individuals within the team, acting as if they were each stake-holder group in turn, and considering all the advantages and disadvantages arising from team objectives, strategies, processes or proposed changes. All possible advantages and disadvantages in relation to the stake-holder group are listed (see the example on page 44). Then the proposed objective or change is modified in order to minimize the disadvantages to the

STAKE-HOLDER ANALYSIS IN PRACTICE

1. Proposed change

A large primary health care team which has always been run along traditional lines has proposed that it will become a fund-holding practice, more like a self-governing team responsible for its own finances and administration. This proposal constitutes a major shift in team practice and philosophy. Who are the major stake-holders?

2. Identify stakeholders

Patients, patients' relatives and carers, practice nurses, doctors, other staff, the community, professional associations, practice administrators and managers.

3. Advantages and disadvantages of the change

Patients

Possible advantages: improved speed of service; improved quality of care; improved administration.

Possible disadvantages: the practice has more concern with money than with patients; competition may lead to poorer-quality care.

Doctors

Possible advantages: better facilities; quicker decision-making; more control over resources.

Possible disadvantages: loss of medical emphasis; administrators will be more concerned with money than with patient care; specialist areas and equipment will be neglected in the interests of satisfying large-scale demand.

Practice Managers

Possible advantages: more power; better quality decision-making; clearer managerial responsibilities.

Possible disadvantages: greater accountability; need to generate income; conflict with hospitals or other fund-holding practices.

4. Adapting the change

Having identified potential advantages and disadvantages from the point of view of each stake-holder group, the team then considers how the change can be modified to meet the various concerns, or how the process of change could be managed appropriately to reduce resistance.

stake-holder group and/or maximize the advantages. This is done for every major stake-holder in turn.

Any final objective or proposed change can be strengthened by such careful consideration of its effects upon the various stake-holders. The technique may also alert the team to conflicts which can then be dealt with using appropriate conflict-handling techniques (see Chapter 6).

MINORITY GROUP INFLUENCE IN TEAMS

Many people in large organizations believe that they cannot bring about changes which they see as necessary and valuable. Research on minority group influence suggests otherwise.

Minority group influence is the process whereby a minority (in terms of number or power) within a team or society brings about enduring change in the attitudes and behaviour of the majority. Exposure to minority group influence appears to cause changes in attitudes in the direction of the 'deviant view', but it also produces more creative thinking about issues, as a result of the cognitive or social conflict generated by the minority. Social psychological research on minority influence therefore has exciting implications for understanding organizational behaviour.

Traditionally only majorities in groups and organizations have been assumed to achieve control, usually through conformity processes. However, Serge Moscovici, a French social psychologist, has argued that minorities also have a significant impact upon the thinking and behaviour of those with whom they interact. Repeated exposure to a consistent minority view leads to marked and internalized changes in attitudes and behaviours. When people conform to a majority view they generally comply publicly without necessarily changing their private beliefs, as we saw earlier. Minorities, in contrast, appear to produce a shift in private views rather than mere public compliance. Moreover, some evidence suggests that even if they do not cause the majority to adopt their viewpoints, minorities encourage greater creativity in thinking about the specific issues they raise. Moscovici argues that minority group influence can be seen in the impact on public attitudes of the environmental and feminist movements in the 1970s and 1980s.

In one early study of minority influence, participants were shown blue and green slides and asked to categorize them accordingly. Those in the experimental group were exposed to a minority of people who consistently categorized some blue slides as green. This procedure had no impact on the majority's correct categorizing of the blue slides. However, when members of the majority were subsequently asked to rate some ambiguous 'blue-green' slides, over half identified the slides in a direction consistent with the minority view. A control group who were not exposed to a minority showed no such effects.

Charlan Nemeth, of the University of Berkeley in California, suggests that minority influence leads to both creative and independent thinking. In one study, participants were exposed to a minority of people who consistently judged blue stimuli as green. Subsequently, the same group were placed in a situation where a *majority* incorrectly rated red stimuli as orange. But the experimental group showed almost complete independence and did not differ significantly from control subjects, who made their judgements of the red stimuli alone. Those not exposed to minority dissent first agreed with the majority's incorrect judgement of orange in over 70 percent of trials. Minorities therefore appear to encourage independence of thinking in those around them.

In a further study of originality, individuals were exposed to a minority who consistently rated blue slides as green. They were then asked to respond seven times in a word association exercise to the words 'blue' or 'green'. Those exposed to a minority judgement gave significantly more word associations and with a higher degree of originality than those exposed to a majority view. Charlan Nemeth concludes that:

> *This work argues for the importance of minority dissent, even dissent that is wrong. Further, we assume that its import lies not in the truth of its position or even in the likelihood that it will prevail. Rather it appears to stimulate divergent thoughts. Issues and problems are considered from more perspectives, and on balance, people detect new solutions and find more correct answers.*

This is essentially a positive, optimistic message which argues that where a minority within the team is powerfully committed to a particular change, by persistence, it can achieve greater creativity in team thinking around the issue, albeit at the price of unpopularity and some conflict. Thus the exploration of opposing opinions and a concern with excellence have been emphasized as essential elements in team effectiveness. The next chapter goes a step further and considers the factors which promote quality of decision-making, creativity and adaptability.

BRINGING ABOUT CHANGE: A MINORITY INFLUENCE STRATEGY

1. The minority needs a clear and well-developed vision of the purpose and outcome of the change. Ideally this might be summarized in a single statement. It is the attractive, appealing and well-justified content of this vision statement which, by repetition, is likely to bring about the conversion of others in the team who were initially opposed to the new proposals.

2. A minority viewpoint is more likely to be accepted by the majority if it is argued coherently and consistently. Therefore, the minority should develop carefully, and repeatedly rehearse the content of the vision as well as the plan for achieving it. Moreover, individuals should ensure that they have at least one ally in the team who will also argue the case. Minorities of two are many more times effective that a minority of one. The greater the degree of unanimity and commitment to the change, the more likely is it to be effected.

3. It requires stamina to maintain the change process in the face of frequent set-backs and stiff opposition.

4. In order to manage resistance the minority in the team need to consider carefully all possible objections to the change and build into their arguments ways of responding positively and convincingly. This may mean modifying plans accordingly beforehand (see the section on stake-holder analysis above). Their counter arguments should thus be convincing and well-rehearsed. At the same time it is important to listen actively to other members of the team and be seen to listen to their concerns.

5. Information dissemination is also important in the change process since much resistance is generated by misunderstanding. The minority in a team can try to ensure that coherent and convincing arguments are presented to all other team members. In summary they must **prepare, rehearse, present** *and* **present** again.

6. If possible the team leader should be committed to and thoroughly rehearsed in the arguments for the change.

– continued

┌─ *continued* ─┐

However, in the absence of support from those hierarchically superior, consistency of argument and repeated presentation is likely to lead to change over time, though at the price of conflict and unpopularity.

7. Participation in the change process is the single most effective way of reducing resistance. This may be accomplished by team meetings and sharing of information. It should also be a real attempt to get the views of others in the team about how the changes might be accomplished most effectively and what the major obstacles are likely to be.

Case Study: A major hospital management team

❑ *The Palmwood Hospital management team consisted of a General Manager, Head of Nursing Services, Director of Surgery, Accountant and Public Works Director. It was a well-established, cohesive and supportive team. When data from a questionnaire study which they had commissioned was fed back to them they were pleased with the results, but noticed that their team was described as having few disagreements, little concern with high standards of performance, critical appraisal and monitoring of colleagues' performance. The team had also voiced anxiety about resistance they were meeting in the hospital when trying to implement changes.*

It was then agreed among the management team that they look at how they managed criticism and disagreement within the team (the climate of excellence) and resistance outside the team (participation). Information-sharing practices were also considered. Initially they were asked to consider the ways they monitored their performance and checked their decision-making. Team members were surprised at the requests since the questionnaire results had shown they worked well as a team. It became clear during the feedback meeting that this aim of team loyalty and cohesiveness sometimes overrode finding the best solution to problems. This also accounted for the negative reactions from other hospital staff they encountered when implementing management decisions. Team members agreed to ensure they became more visible on the 'shop floor' and to use feedback from staff to appraise decisions made within the team.

They successfully used stake-holder analysis to step out of their roles as team members and to think more creatively about problems. The method also enabled the team to anticipate and therefore reduce resistance from other staff groups.

Chapter Five

Creative Problem-Solving

It has become a cliché to speak of the rapid change in society. Organizations change with bewildering frequency as they are privatized, acquired, rationalized, restructured, reorganized or liquidated. One major cause of this rapid change is the external socio-economic environment within which organizations find themselves. Competition has become a global rather than a national phenomenon. Organizations have become international rather than national. Moreover, the demands of consumers are shifting constantly as people require new and different commodities and services to meet their needs. Information technology has also made the environment much more demanding.

If we lived in a climate where the weather changed constantly from hour to hour, sometimes hot, sometimes wet, sometimes cold, sometimes snowing, we would need to be prepared for every eventuality and adapt quickly. We might need raincoats, cool clothes, umbrellas, warm clothes and even the occasional shelter as we made our way around. Similarly in their rapidly changing environment, organizations need to be highly adaptable. This requires that organizations are innovative. Just as human beings have adapted to their environments by finding new and improved ways of organizing societies and work, so organizations too must be innovative in order to survive.

In response to complexity and change many organizations have made the team the functional unit of the organization. Instead of individuals being responsible for separate pieces of work, groups of individuals come together to combine their efforts, knowledge and skills to achieve shared goals. Consequently, for organizations to be innovative, teams also must be innovative, adaptable and essentially creative in their response to problems both within their organizations and in the wider environment.

TEAM INNOVATION

Figure 3 shows a model of team innovation which emphasizes the importance of some principal factors examined in earlier chapters. The model demonstrates how shared vision, commitment to excellence, participative safety and support for innovation, all determine the level of a team's innovativeness. Innovation is defined here as

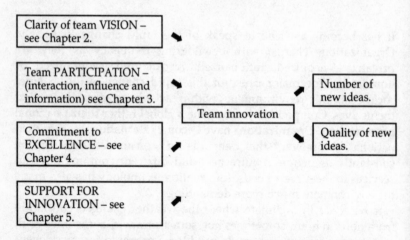

Figure 3: A model of team innovation

the introduction of new and improved ways of doing things by a team. Creativity and innovation are distinguished in the following ways: creativity refers to new ideas and their development; and innovation includes creativity but also requires that creative ideas are put into action, within a group, organization or society.

1. Vision/shared objectives
It was shown in Chapter 2 that vision partly determines the effectiveness of groups at work. But there is also strong evidence that a clearly stated mission is important in predicting success in innovation. In a major research study of 418 project teams it was found that a clearly stated mission predicted success at each stage

of the innovation process, i.e. conception, planning, execution and termination.

HOW INNOVATIVE IS YOUR TEAM AT WORK?

EXERCISE 5

Compared with other similar teams how innovative do you consider your team to be? Circle the appropriate response for the following task areas:

	Highly stable: few changes introduced	Highly innovative: some changes introduced		Highly innovative: many changes introduced
Setting work targets or objectives.	1	2	3	4	5
Deciding the methods used to achieve objective/targets.	1	2	3	4	5
Initiating new procedures or information systems.	1	2	3	4	5
Developing innovative ways of accomplishing targets/objectives	1	2	3	4	5
Initiating changes in the job content and work methods of your staff.	1	2	3	4	5

Total score ☐

Administer this questionnaire to all members of your team and calculate the average level of innovation. If the team scores above an average of 3.5, team members will be likely to see the team as innovative. Scores at 3 or below should be considered an indication that the team might be more adaptive. However, this should be considered carefully in the context of the team's work. For example, in a hospital, highly innovative surgical teams might not be what is required if standard operating procedures should always be followed. Therefore, when analysing the questionnaire it is important to bear in mind the context within which the team is working.

2. Participative safety

Cohesiveness is a rather amorphous concept and has generally shown inconsistent relationships with group effectiveness, as was described in Chapter 4. However, high levels of participation are associated with low resistance to change and high levels of innovation in teams. The more people participate in team decision-making through having influence, interacting with those involved in change processes, and sharing information, the more likely are they to invest in the outcomes of those decisions and to offer ideas for new and improved ways of working.

The level of safety in the group is also important, since work group members are more likely to take the risk of proposing new ways of working in a climate which they see as non-threatening and supportive. There is certainly evidence that amongst teams of scientists, innovation is high when the atmosphere within the team is seen as warm, supportive, but intellectually demanding.

3. Commitment to excellence

In the last chapter we saw how 'groupthink' and 'process losses' can reduce the effectiveness of group performance and group decision-making. Similarly, highly cohesive groups may inhibit attempts at innovation by treating them as deviations from group norms and practices. High levels of participative safety alone might lead to a reluctance to challenge poor or even potentially dangerous plans for innovation on the basis that such challenges would represent a threat to the team's warm, interpersonal climate. Indeed, it has been argued that minority group influence leads to high levels of conflict but is a major cause of innovation in teams. In other words, those who want to introduce innovations in teams risk conflict and so may avoid innovation in order to maintain the harmony of the group.

Commitment to excellence is characterized by a shared concern with quality of performance and by the existence of systems for evaluation, modification, control and critical appraisal. Improved task orientation will produce innovation by encouraging diversity and creativity, whilst at the same time ensuring high quality of innovation via the careful examination of ideas proposed.

4. Support for innovation

Finally, the idea of norms or support for innovation is the expectation, approval and practical support of attempts to introduce new and improved ways of doing things in the work environment. Within groups, new ideas may be rejected or ignored, or they may find verbal and active support from other team members.

Many groups in organizations, as part of their overall objectives, may express support for the development of new and improved ways of working, but they may not actually provide the practical support to enable ideas to be put into practice. Certainly some organizational psychologists have shown how organizations have theories espoused (the way that they say they work) and theories in use (the way that they actually work). High levels of both verbal and practical support will lead to more attempts to introduce innovations in teams. Verbal support is most helpful when team members initially propose ideas. Practical support can take the form of co-operation in the development of ideas as well as the provision of time and resources by group members to apply them.

Some teams have difficulty providing even verbal support for innovation however. But, if people seem inherently resistant to new ideas then teams are likely to propose only those ideas they feel sure about. Minimizing risk by not giving verbal support often means minimising innovation. A simple technique a team can use to promote support and openness to new ideas in meetings is the 'yes, and . . .' method (see below).

THE 'YES AND . . .' METHOD

People often look for faults in a new idea when it is first raised. This can have the effect of reducing enthusiasm and the preparedness of people to offer new ideas. The 'yes and . . .' method is a way of avoiding the 'no,' and 'yes, but . . .' traps which are often the end of a new idea. Try saying 'yes,' and then building on the idea in a meeting before deciding that it will not work. Try to build on the positive or add your own positive idea to the suggestion. This is a simple but very powerful technique, which, if applied as a rule in departmental meetings, can change the climate substantially. It also enables group members to identify quickly the person who finds it hardest not to slip back into 'yes, but . . .' ways.

CREATIVE PROBLEM-SOLVING IN TEAMS

We tend to think of problem-solving as being a single activity, but a good deal of research indicates that there are a number of distinct and important stages. Each requires different kinds of skills and activities. It is therefore useful to distinguish between the different stages, and to use appropriate skills for each. Four well-established stages are: problem exploration, developing alternative ideas, selecting an option, and implementing the preferred option:

Stage 1 – Exploration
↓
Stage 2 – Ideation
↓
Stage 3 – Selection
↓
Stage 4 – Implementation

Stage 1 – Exploration

Probably the most important stage of team problem-solving is the clarification and exploration of a problem. It is characteristic of decision-making in teams that people usually begin to try to develop solutions to problems before clarifying and exploring and, if necessary, re-defining the problem itself. But the more time spent in exploring and clarifying a problem before attempting to seek solutions, the better the quality of the ultimate solution. Moreover, the time saved by careful exploration of problems almost always outweighs the time expended on this task. Problem exploration can take the form of goal orientation or stake-holder analysis (see Chapter 4).

Stage 2 – Ideation

Having suspended attempts at solution development during Stage 1, the next step is to develop a range of alternative solutions to the problem as defined. When making decisions, teams generally seek for 'one way out'. One idea is proposed and the team goes with that idea, making appropriate modifications as are perceived necessary. However, research on team problem-solving suggests that it is most effective to begin by generating a range of possible solutions. This is the stage when having a safe climate with verbal support for innovation and using 'yes, and . . .' responses is particularly important to promote a sense of confidence. During this phase also, all critical judgements should be suspended. Techniques such as brainstorming are best used (techniques which are described later in this chapter) and it should be a stage which is both playful and challenging, when all ideas are welcomed and encouraged.

Stage 3 – Selection
In this stage the aim is to encourage constructive controversy about appropriate ways forward. It is necessary and desirable to be critical and judgemental, but this needs to be done in a way which is essentially constructive and personally supportive. If Stage 2 has generated many solutions, it may be necessary to select the three or four solutions which appear most promising, but it is important to avoid selecting simply those which fit. At least one potential solution should be something which involves a completely new way of dealing with the issue. In relation to each idea a stake-holder analysis and/or a negative brainstorming session can be conducted. These techniques are designed to enable people to anticipate the likely reactions to proposed solutions. Negative brainstorming also helps to seek out in a constructive way, all possible defects in the solution suggested, and to remedy these by building on new ideas.

This stage of critical analysis and selection in the team is important because there is a danger a team may select a solution simply because it is a solution rather than because it is the *best* solution. In an eagerness to achieve 'closure' and avoid further uncertainty or ambiguity, teams are sometimes too prepared to overlook problems inherent in solutions they have adopted. Another method of encouraging critical analysis of solutions within teams is to appoint a 'devil's advocate' within the group (see Chapter 4).

Stage 4 – Implementation
If the other three stages have been conducted carefully, implementation should be the least difficult and most rewarding stage of the problem-solving process. During this stage, teams should be open to possible teething problems that arise and be prepared to modify the implementation process appropriately. At the same time, the implementation stage should also be managed in a way that ensures that the original idea is implemented rather than watered down once realities are faced. It is sometimes too easy to lose the

courage of our convictions and go for a compromise which does not really satisfy anyone in the team. At the implementation stage, the innovator should gain support in the form of resources, time and co-operation, from others outside the team who may have influence on the effectiveness of the implementation process.

These then are four distinct stages of problem-solving. Next are described a set of techniques or methods which can be applied at the different stages of creative problem-solving.

TECHNIQUES FOR PROMOTING CREATIVITY WITHIN A TEAM

Described below are various techniques designed to help generate new and different ideas in any area of team work activity. However, it is important to recognize that these techniques are simply aids and are not themselves magical sources of solutions. Creativity is 95 percent hard work and 5 percent serendipitous discovery. Therefore, when teams use these techniques it is necessary to put in a good deal of effort to see how the ideas that they generate can help practically in dealing with the situation the team faces. What will not work is a passive approach which assumes that the right answers will just appear as a result of using the techniques.

These creativity techniques are intended to provide new and different ways of looking at the issues that teams face, and wild, 'off the wall' alternatives to existing methods of dealing with challenges.

Technique 1 – classical brainstorming

In classical brainstorming, group members produce as many ideas as possible, even Utopian or fantastic ideas. The aim is to produce a large quantity of ideas, not necessarily to worry about quality. Judgements are suspended and participants are urged to accept all ideas offered. Group members are also encouraged to use each other's ideas to stimulate more new ideas and this is called 'piggy-backing'. So the essential guide-lines are:

- quantity of ideas
- judgements suspended
- piggy-backing.

There are a number of ways in which brainstorming can be conducted in groups. One is to go round the group asking each member in turn for an idea, thus encouraging quieter group members to participate. Many prefer a less structured approach where group members call out ideas randomly. However, the best way to conduct brainstorming is to give group members an opportunity to generate ideas alone and to write them down before bringing them to the group setting. At this point piggy-backing can occur. The advantage of everyone returning to the group is that it can bring team members together in fruitful social interaction, and confers a sense of participation and involvement in the generation of new ideas for change.

Classical brainstorming is used by many groups, but the most frequent mistake is the failure to suspend judgement while ideas are being proposed. During the idea-generation phase of problem-solving, critical judgement must be withheld. It is also valuable to encourage new wild and quite different ideas in the brainstorming process, rather than brainstorming simply within the current paradigm of the group. Above all there should be an element of fun in brainstorming. It is sometimes the wildest, craziest ideas, that contain within them the seed of a very different and productive new approach to the task or issue which the group is facing.

Technique 2 – brainwriting pool

This technique is a variant of classical brainstorming which builds on the superior performance of individuals over groups in brainstorms (see Chapter 1) and has the effect of generating very large numbers of ideas, within a short space of time. Group members, seated around a table, are given blank sheets of paper with space to record ideas. After generating five or ten ideas the sheets are placed in the middle of the table. Each member then continues writing more ideas on the sheets filled in by other group members. They are urged particularly to piggy-back upon the ideas that others have already developed. A session of 20 minutes can produce literally hundreds of ideas from within a group. Redundancy is reduced because all participants can see the ideas produced by others. Furthermore, group members, while receiving stimulation from the ideas of other members of the group, can proceed at their own pace.

This is a system which can be used when members of the group find it difficult to get together at the same time. Ideas sheets can be circulated and added to over a period of days. A productive variant of this technique is one made possible by computer networking systems. 'Brain-netting' involves setting up a file in a network system to which all group members have access. The problem or issue is headlined at the top of the file and then group members simply add their ideas or suggestions to those of their colleagues within the file. Group members do not need to be together to conduct the brainstorm; moreover, they all have a record of the ongoing outcomes of the process. This is a highly productive process which involves a minimum of effort from group members.

Technique 3 – negative brainstorming

This technique has been described fully in chapter 4 and can be used very effectively to improve creatively on existing or proposed objectives, strategies, work methods or processes.

Technique 4 – goal orientation

Goal orientation is a way of restating problems or objectives in order to find more creative perspectives from which to view them. This in turn can lead to creative solutions or objectives.

Technique 5 – table of elements

The table of elements is a technique for breaking a problem or issue down into a set of elements or components, brainstorming within each, and then choosing from among the various components those ideas which seem most promising or creative in taking the team forward. It generates an enormous number of potential solutions to a problem in a very short space of time. However, it is only suitable for problems or issues which can be broken down into components and elements.

❑ **Example.** The team has tried to come up with an idea for a novel social event which will bring people together and help them to have a good time outside work. The elements of this problem could be identified as: the people who will come to the event; where the event will be held; what activities will take place; when the event will be held; what the purpose of the event will be. The group then brainstorms ideas under each of these elements, or headings (see the table on page 60). The next stage involves choosing potentially wild or promising ideas from among the many combinations of possibilities generated by the table of elements. In this exercise it is worth throwing in quite different ideas within each part of the brainstorm in order to enable group members to break out of existing ways of thinking. Participants can also choose an array of items from within the elements purely at random (i.e. stick a pin in each column to produce a novel combination). Inevitably, such strategies generate solutions which may appear outlandish or nonsensical at first sight. The purpose of these exercises is, however, to stimulate new ways of looking at problems and this provides 5 percent of the creativity. The other 95 percent comes from the team in seeking to make the wild idea into a workable option. For example, if the following items are selected

- *children only*
- *Bahamas*
- *treasure hunt*
- *weekend*
- *learning to swim*

it is possible to combine them into the following more practical solution:

At the social event at a swimming pool, an activity especially designed for the children of team members could be arranged (children only). It could involve a game of pirates (learning to swim), looking for gold tokens (treasure hunt) on a treasure island (Bahamas).

The process of using the table of elements takes only 10 or 15 minutes to complete, but can generate literally tens of thousands of ideas within that time.

Technique 6 – stake-holder analysis

This is described in Chapter 4 and is a way of thinking through change proposals or team objectives from the perspectives of those principally affected by the group's work. It can provide valuable direction for teams in modifying change proposals or objectives appropriately.

USING CREATIVITY TECHNIQUES IN GROUP MEETINGS

It takes courage to attempt to use these creativity techniques in team meetings. Like any new idea it will be responded to by some with only half-hearted support, ridicule, or even outright resistance. All creativity and innovation involves taking risks and if

Table of elements: A novel social event

People	Place	Activities	Time	Purpose
Team members	Restaurant	Raise money for charity	Weekend	Learning to swim
Team members and partners	Park	Get to know each other	Friday evening	
Children only	Boat	Have a good time		
Team members and customers	Paris			
Visually impaired children	Bahamas	Treasure hunt		As a reward
Partners only	Motorway	Learn new language		
Team members' pets	Beach	Play golf		
	Swimming pool	Play tennis		
	Hotel			
	Theatre			

the team is persistent and confident in introducing the techniques they will work. It is rather like jumping off a high diving board: you have to have a go at it and take the plunge. In groups you have to keep trying in order to develop confidence in using new techniques.

It can often be helpful to string together a number of these creative techniques. How this is done is itself an opportunity to be creative. It is important, however, to remember the importance of the four steps of problem-solving mentioned above when putting a group session together, i.e., exploration, ideation, selection, and implementation.

It is also helpful to think carefully about how time in group meetings will be used and which creativity techniques will be tried. Sufficient time needs to be allocated for each technique so that the team is not too rushed and each technique does not take too long to complete. Make sure the team has appointed a facilitator who understands the use of the techniques and does the job of a facilitator rather than dictates or controls. Make sure that there are sufficient materials for recording ideas, such as flip charts and overhead projectors.

In recording people's ideas in a team, the facilitator should (whenever possible) write exactly what the individual has said. It is appropriate occasionally to paraphrase a particularly long contribution, but this should only be done with the agreement of the individual who has made the proposal. Check the wording with them and see that they are happy with what you have produced. Try to note every contribution, especially those that are humorous or throw-away comments, since they can be a good source of creative ideas. To help create the right sort of climate in a group for creativity it is useful to agree some ground rules before getting started. These can be posted on a flip chart to act as a reminder throughout the session.

Ground rules will vary according to the particular aims of the team. A typical set of ground rules for a creative session might well include:

- be concise

- show interest and support

- jot down all stray thoughts

- suspend judgement

- say 'yes and . . .', rather than 'yes but . . .'
- take risks – include the unusual and strange.

If the flow of ideas is drying up, try taking a creative break from the problem. There are numerous ways of doing this, such as word association games, going out for walks, story telling, etc.

OTHER INFLUENCES ON TEAM INNOVATION

Teams do not exist in isolation and the factors which determine the creativity of teams are going to be multiple and varied. However, extensive research conducted by myself and colleagues at the University of Sheffield has indicated that the climate of the team – vision, participative safety, task orientation and support for innovation – principally determines the level of team innovation. But four other factors are also important:

Resources
Contrary to popular belief, the level of team resources seems to bear little relationship to innovativeness and creativity. In our work with management teams in the UK National Health Service we studied teams with budgets ranging from £6 million to £47 million per year. There was no relationship between team budget and level of innovativeness. Similar results have been found in studies of more than 1,000 scientific research teams worldwide.

Team size
Research on the relationship between team size and creativity shows that larger teams are less creative. This may be simply because as teams grow the effectiveness of communication processes is diminished and problems of co-ordination increase. In general the maximum team size for relatively high levels of creativity is between ten and twelve people.

Lifetime of the team
Our research with hospital management teams suggests that the longer teams have been together the more effective they are in implementing innovations within the organization. The number of innovations does not appear to be a function of team longevity. However, we noted that the effectiveness of the innovations applied within the hospital setting tends to be higher the longer the

— HOW INNOVATIVE ARE YOU AT WORK? —

EXERCISE 6

The following questionnaire explores your feelings about innovation and change at work. How far do you agree or disagree with the following statements (indicate the appropriate number)?

	Strongly disagree 1	Disagree 2	Not sure 3	Agree 4	Strongly agree 5
I try to introduce improved methods of doing things at work.	[ ]	[ ]	[ ]	[ ]	[ ]
I have ideas which significantly improve the way the job is done.	[ ]	[ ]	[ ]	[ ]	[ ]
I suggest new working methods to the people I work with.	[ ]	[ ]	[ ]	[ ]	[ ]
I contribute to changes in the way my team works.	[ ]	[[ ]	[ ]	[ ]	[ ]
I am receptive to new ideas which I can use to improve things at work.	[ ]	[ ]	[ ]	[ ]	[ ]

The average score for 250 employed males and females on this scale was 19.0. If you score 20 or over you have a high propensity to innovate. Take the average score for your team to determine whether your team has a high or low propensity to innovate. If the average score is high, it is more likely the team will produce creative ideas.

team have been together (though one caveat to this is that the teams we studied had rarely been together for more than two years). Some researchers have argued that if teams are together for much longer they become less creative, because team members achieve too comfortable a consensus in their views of the world and consequently fail to generate new and improved ways of doing things.

Individual factors
Individuals who have high work autonomy (i.e. freedom in how to do their jobs) and who are confident and intelligent tend to have high levels of creativity. In our research we found that teams comprised of innovative individuals (i.e. people who have a high tendency to introduce new and improved ways of doing things at work), are likely to be innovative also.

THE CHANGE PROCESS

This chapter has examined ways in which teams can promote innovation and creativity in order to remain adaptable and effective within their organizations. In one major research study of over 2,000 male and female British managers conducted by Professor Nigel Nicholson and myself, it was found that the vast majority had introduced new and improved ways of doing things when they changed jobs (Nicholson and West, 1988). They changed the objectives of their jobs, the methods, scheduling, practices, procedures and even who they dealt with and how they dealt with them. It is significant that in the job changing process, people moving into existing jobs are highly innovative – moulding and improving the jobs to fit their way of doing things. Moreover people who have the opportunity to be innovative at work, introducing new and improved ways of doing things, are far more satisfied with their jobs than those who do not have such opportunities. It was a remarkable finding in the study that, among those who took a job move leading to reduced opportunities for innovation, the negative effects upon their mental health were greater even than amongst those managers and professionals who had become unemployed.

The opportunity to be creative and innovative at work is central to our well-being. This is true, not just of managerial and professional workers, but of manual workers too. Recent research has shown that one of the greatest causes of stress for assembly line workers is lack of autonomy and control, which inhibits creativity.

The conclusion from the research is that the need to be creative and innovative is a major source of satisfaction for us at work. The research also indicates that teams have an overwhelming influence on the extent to which people are able to be creative in their workplace – that a team climate supportive of innovation is crucial. It is through attention to creating a climate in which people are clear about their objectives, have a sense of safety with their fellow team members, experience high levels of participation, and emphasize excellence in the work that the individual desire to innovate is translated into practical team outcomes, which promote both team effectiveness and team member well-being.

Chapter Six

Team Support

Teams play important roles in enabling people to cope with every-day work challenges and in providing social and emotional support which contributes to the quality of their lives, both at work and more generally. There are important differences in the job-related mental health of those who undertake demanding and monotonous tasks between those who do and those who do not have opportunities for social contact with work colleagues. Those who can chat to and joke with other workers suffer fewer problems of job-related mental health than those who, because of noise or the design of their jobs, are unable to enjoy conversation with those around them. Team support is therefore an important element in conceptions of team effectiveness. For example, those in the caring professions can derive particular support from their team member colleagues in coping with the stress associated with their work.

Below we examine the four principal social dimensions of team working. Practical ways of improving team functioning on those dimensions are also described. They are social support, conflict resolution, support for growth and development and social climate. Each of these dimensions contributes to team member well-being and long term team viability, as indicated in Figure 4.

SOCIAL SUPPORT

It is useful to think of four types of social support: emotional, instrumental, informational and appraisal and then to distinguish between articulated and enacted support.

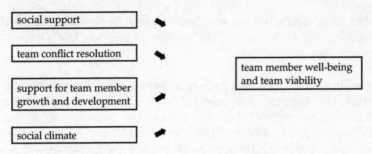

Figure 4: The social dimensions of team working

EMOTIONAL SUPPORT

This is the kind of social support which we most readily identify. It is the notion of a shoulder to cry on, an encouraging word and sympathetic understanding of another's emotional pain:

Case example

❑ *Louise, a health visitor, had been visiting one particular family on an intensive basis. The family had a baby, Jonathan, who was at some risk of cot death. On Tuesday morning she arrived in her office to be told that baby Jonathan had been rushed to the Accident and Emergency Department in the early hours of the morning, only to be pronounced dead on arrival. The child had all the classic signs of sudden infant death.*

Louise was shocked and upset and immediately called her manager to inform her of the tragic event. Her manager listened briefly to what Louise had to say, then informed her of the steps that she must take to inform the Health Authority and of the importance of writing up her notes very quickly. The manager told Louise that they may get a chance to talk again in a couple of weeks when she next visited Louise's locality. Louise put down the phone and felt a mixture of grief and frustration. Her grief and emotional burden had not been lessened. On the contrary, they had been added to and complicated by a frustration with her manager demanding immediate bureaucratic action in response to the event.

One of Louise's colleagues then arrived in the office and knowing how frequently Louise had been visiting Jonathan and his family, said she sympathized, acknowledging how terribly upset Louise must have felt that this should happen. Louise then began to cry and her colleague put an arm around her in comfort.

Later in the day they met to talk again and the colleague, by listening and being supportive, enabled Louise to talk about her own feelings of guilt that she had not done enough to prevent the cot death. Louise felt guilty at not being more assertive in insisting that the baby should be admitted for observation and nutritional support. By expressing the guilt and discussing the feelings with her colleague, Louise was helped to work through these feelings.

Here is an example of a colleague providing emotional support when the support was needed, and on a continuing basis. Emotional support involves being an active, open listener. It does not involve giving advice or direction, rather it is simply providing the space within which people can express their emotions. It also involves a sense of caring towards the person receiving the support. Louise's colleague understood the grief she must feel and enabled her to express that by acknowledging it openly, placing her arms around her and giving her permission to cry. Finally, the colleague offered the opportunity for continued emotional support rather than withdrawing too swiftly.

To what extent should team members provide emotional support for non-work-related difficulties such as marital difficulties, death in the family, illness, or financial problems? If a colleague is experiencing such emotional difficulties as a result of their lives outside work, it is often desirable and necessary that team colleagues should provide support. However, a line has to be drawn between team members offering appropriate and valuable emotional support to colleagues and delving inappropriately into one another's private lives without invitation in ways which might undermine work relationships. There is no simple rule since it depends very much on relationships between team members and the particular circumstances in which people find themselves. However, involvement in a team member's personal life should only happen where there is a clear invitation or request from that team member. Sometimes colleagues at work can appear somewhat predatory in their desire to involve themselves in the emotional lives of those around them. This can be destructive for individuals as well as potentially damaging to working relationships.

There are some emotional difficulties which require professional help. Where a team member has become frequently or deeply depressed; where problems of drug abuse or alcoholism are evident; or where an individual appears suicidal, team members should generally recommend to such colleagues that they seek professional advice and help. It is important that team members recognize the limitations of their competence in providing emotional support rather than attempting to provide professional counselling. Many organizations now employ the services of a counsellor or a counselling agency, however, and these should usually be a first rather than a last resort.

INFORMATIONAL SUPPORT
Social support is not only about being warm, empathic and caring. It is also about doing practical things to aid team members:

Case example:
❑ *Sarah, the practice nurse in a primary health care team, had been given responsibility for regularly checking up on the case of David, a 12 year-old anorexic boy. But as she was becoming increasingly anxious about David's weight loss and depression, she went to speak with Kate, one of the general practitioners. Kate was sympathetic and listened attentively to Sarah's anxieties. At the same time the GP advised Sarah to contact the Atkinson Morley Hospital which specializes in the treatment of eating disorders. Kate suggested that Sarah talk with the head of the relevant department at the Hospital to see whether the child should be admitted. Sarah was able to use Kate's information about the name of the hospital, the specialist and their telephone number in order to make contact and get expert advice. As a consequence, Sarah's anxiety was somewhat relieved and she was given practical means for aiding David in his illness.*

In this case it is clear that informational social support can have important consequences. The extent to which team members provide each other with informational support of this kind is an important element in the overall social supportiveness of the team.

INSTRUMENTAL SUPPORT
Instrumental support refers to the practical, 'doing' support that team members offer to one another.

❑ *Jenny, a teacher, had received a call from her childminder to say that her daughter was unwell. She wanted to go home quickly, but had another lesson before the end of school which she was reluctant to cancel because of important work that the children were due to do. Her colleague, overhearing the conversation, offered to take the final class for her, enabling Jenny to go home.*

❑ *A receptionist in a primary health care team was overloaded with paperwork as she tried to put together the medical notes of patients due to see the GPs and the practice nurse that morning. Her colleague, seeing her overloaded, then took half of the pile in order to relieve her of some of the work.*

❑ *A researcher needed to find an organization within which she could try out a questionnaire she was developing which looked at team effectiveness in organizations. Her colleague telephoned three or four different people he knew in different organizations whom he thought might be willing to provide access for her to conduct her questionnaire study. He negotiated with each and, finding one who was willing, then provided the name and address to the researcher.*

These are all examples of instrumental support where one team member provides practical action to aid another in achieving the goals that they were aiming for. This may occur in a situation of crisis or simply as part of routine work. Social support in whatever form and at whatever time has an important impact upon the social climate, the well-being of team members and the viability of a team.

APPRAISAL SUPPORT

Appraisal support is the help individual team members can provide one another in making sense of a particular problem situation. As described in the previous chapter, problem definition is the most important stage of problem-solving. Team members therefore can provide useful social support by helping their colleagues in the process of appraising particular problem situations. Ideally, this need not involve offering solutions, but rather examines a range of alternative appraisals of any given problem situations.

❑ *Many individuals are faced by job insecurity in the 1990s and Chris was one of them. He had worked in the same organization for the last 15 years but suddenly found that the future of the organization was in jeopardy as its performance had not matched expectations. He then talked with two of his team colleagues about his own future as they discussed possible options. They suggested that there were two or three career possibilities within the parent organization for him, but also that there may be other better opportunities outside. They offered appraisals of the situation which ranged from the most threatening, i.e. unemployment, through to seeing the situation as one which was full of potential and promise for Chris (since it may give him the opportunity to specialize in areas which previously had been denied him because of the demands of the organization). Chris began to see that there were important positive opportunities in the situation which was not as threatening as he had first thought. He decided to explore with much more vigour the various alternatives open to him.*

Here is an example of an individual whose colleagues provided appraisal support which enabled him to deal with his predicament in a constructive and positive way and which may also have had important positive implications for him in the future. The way colleagues within teams help us to appraise situations can therefore be an important contributor to the overall social climate of the team.

The more that team members provide and enact support of all kinds – informational, instrumental, emotional and appraisal – the more cohesive and supportive the team becomes. In the long run, the mental health of team members is thereby improved, since we know there is a strong and positive relationship between social support at work and job-related mental health.

TEAM CONFLICT RESOLUTION

In Chapter 4 there was some emphasis on the fact that conflict is not only endemic but desirable in teams. Team conflict can be a source of excellence, quality and creativity. However, occasions can arise where conflict in teams becomes interpersonally destructive and leads to lowered effectiveness. This occurs especially where the conflict takes on a personal quality which results in team members attacking one another, or denigrating each other's skills, abilities or functioning in some way. This is unhealthy both for the individuals concerned and for the team as a whole. Indeed recent research by my colleagues at the University of Sheffield has shown that the single greatest cause of stress and strain at work for people attending a psychotherapy clinic is interpersonal conflict with work colleagues. Although job insecurity or work overload can be major causes of stress, it is often the conflicts with colleagues that keep us awake at night. Why do these occur and what can be done to prevent or overcome them?

Interpersonal conflicts are often not caused by the personalities of the individuals involved, but by work role or organizational factors. There is a tendency to attribute to individuals problems which may be due to factors in the work environment.

❑ *Gwen, a health visitor in a primary health care team, was experiencing repeated conflict with the social worker attached to her team. They tended to disagree over cases of suspected non-accidental injury to children where Gwen felt that the social worker was too ready to involve the courts and the police and was too dismissive of Gwen's knowledge of the families involved. The conflict had escalated to the extent that the two had had a heated disagreement in Gwen's office which was overheard by other members of staff. Gwen accused the social worker of being unfeeling and too autocratic. The social worker responded by telling Gwen that it was not her job to be doing social work and that she should be looking after the physical health of the family. He called her argumentative, interfering and non-communicative and accused her of not being able to work effectively in a team.*

In this case, personalities may not be at the root of the problem. Rather it may be due to a lack of clarity and mutual understanding of roles. There is often conflict between health visitors and social workers in general practice settings. This is usually because the health visitor and the social worker have not spent time exploring and clarifying each other's roles. The social worker may be unaware of the broader role of the health visitor in taking responsibility for all aspects of a family's health and well-being, including the social and emotional aspects. Health visitors, on the other hand, often fail to be sufficiently aware of the statutory responsibilities of social workers who ultimately may 'carry the can' if a tragic event occurs.

Such conflicts can be overcome, not by reference to the particular case, but by a full exploration of each other's roles and some negotiation around how the roles can effectively complement rather than compete with one another. Therefore whenever there is conflict in a team, one of the first things to assess is the extent to which people are clearly aware of each other's roles and the objectives of those roles. (Exercises in role negotiation and role clarification are described in Chapter 8).

The causes of interpersonal conflict in teams can often be due to broader organizational problems such as lack of structure, inadequacy of resources, poor organizational climate or inappropriate organizational strategy. Again, team members may focus on each other's behaviour and personalities to find explanations for difficulties when the causes lie outside the team. A good example of this is the poor relationship which often exists between midwives and junior hospital doctors in hospital settings. Midwives may well have many years of practical experience in obstetric practice. Junior hospital doctors are still training but because they are hierarchically superior to midwives, some may feel intimidated, irritated or resentful of the midwives' extensive and superior experience. For their part, midwives can feel irritated by the directive behaviour of inexperienced doctors. The problem is created by the inappropriateness of the medical hierarchy.

Personality does play an important part in team functioning and in the concept of team roles, as Chapter 1 explored. This is the idea that groups of people have 'team personalities'. Some individuals may be dominant and leader-oriented ('shapers') while others may be more creative (the 'plant' team role). Where there are two or more shapers in a team there may be friction: two dominant people may well hold opposing views about the team's direction. The monitor-evaluator who is keen to ensure that a decision taken by the team is always right and has been thought through carefully will be unmoved by the enthusiasm and certainty of the creative plant in the team. The plant may be irritated by the questioning and lack of enthusiasm of the monitor-evaluator when a new and potentially exciting proposal is put forward. Some of the differences between team members can be due to characteristic styles of working which, while valuable in themselves, may cause some mutual antagonism or friction. Recognition of the value of the variability of styles within teams helps to overcome such difficulties.

There is no doubt, however, that sometimes conflicts between individuals within teams cannot be dismissed as due to role, organizational, or team personality-type factors. Irritations do arise and difficulties do have to be worked through. For the most part people will get on with others with whom they work when that is unavoidable. This is *the psychology of inevitability* – if a child is told that he or she will definitely be sitting next to another particular child in class over the course of the next year (whom he or she has not liked previously), the child's attitude is likely to change. Similarly if we know we have to work with certain individuals who we may have found difficult in the past, we may work harder to find strategies to work more effectively and co-operatively with them. But when conflicts between team members do arise and cannot be managed in ways so far described, how should team members proceed? Brushing major problems under the carpet in a working relationship can be an effective strategy in the short-term but the danger is that frustrations build and will erupt in a single destructive incident. Another book in this series, *Interpersonal Conflicts at Work* by Robert Edelmann has suggested repeatedly the importance of trying to work through interpersonal difficulties when they arise, in a constructive, open way. This means being clear with the other team member about difficulties and conflicts which have arisen and setting aside time to talk them through. Avoiding or denying problems is unlikely to make a long-term contribution to team viability.

There are four ways of reacting to a difficulty which has occurred with another team member. The first is to be *passive*, which means doing nothing and pretending the problem does not exist, but as indicated above this may have long-term detrimental effects such as simmering frustrations which overflow inappropriately.

The second strategy is to be *passively aggressive*, which is perhaps the most destructive strategy of all. This is where the individual avoids the other team member, doesn't talk to him or her, deliberately disagrees with every suggestion made by the other team member, denigrates the other team member to colleagues, or even sabotages his or her work secretly. Such passive-aggressive strategies allow team members no opportunity of reconciling the conflicts or difficulties since they do not involve owning up to the existence of conflict. Passive-aggressive strategies undermine the climate of the whole team and are very destructive to team functioning.

The third approach is to be *aggressive*, attacking the other team member verbally face-to-face with the intention of hurting. Such a strategy is marginally more positive than passive-aggressive or passive approaches since it enables the individual team member to get rid of angry feelings. However, it tends to leave a thick residue of bitterness, resentment and coldness which harms both the team members and the deeper social climate of the team.

The fourth strategy has been called *assertiveness* which involves telling the other individual about one's own feelings and asking for changes in behaviour which may prevent a recurrence of the conflict. The difference between aggressive and assertive statements may be illustrated in the following way:

'You're incompetent and you've wasted a whole week's work for me.' (aggressive statement)

'I feel really upset because I relied on you to make sure this information was posted on time. And I feel upset because all my hard work of the week seems wasted.' (assertive statement)

Assertiveness therefore involves the clear expression of feelings and the use of 'I' rather than 'you' statements. It involves being clear about one's own feelings and wants from the situation, whereas aggressive statements simply involve the intention to hurt.

Assertive discussions therefore demand that both sides try to use 'I' statements in talking about their feelings and in identifying behaviour and the consequences of behaviour. At the same time there is a real desire to identify desired changes in behaviour which will prevent the recurrence of the problem, with a mutual commitment to make those changes.

Where team members are unable to resolve their differences, it may be necessary to involve the team leader (or where the team leader is one of the two protagonists, the team leader's superior). The strategy here should be for the team leader to give each person the opportunity to state their feelings about the issue. Once the feelings of both sides have been expressed, the facts of the case can be dealt with. It is important, however, to try to separate out feelings from facts since the two can be inextricably bound up in a discussion which can then lead to further hostility and misunderstanding. By carefully talking through the facts and feelings, the 'mediator' can enable both sides to present their cases fully and to explore, perhaps without agreeing on an interpretation of previous events, how future difficulties might be avoided. Mediation, therefore, involves four stages:

- explore the feelings of both team members
- explore the facts as perceived by both team members
- agree goals for avoiding a recurrence of the conflict
- agree action plans.

Case example: The retail co-ordination team
❑ *Elaine was the team leader in a retail coordination team of a major oil company. Geoffrey, her newest, youngest, and least-experienced team member, had been with the team for just a year. Elaine then discovered that unknown to her, Geoffrey had been conducting work with a number of retail outlets in a nearby town using the team's resources, at the same time as conducting the major project for which he was employed. When Elaine expressed outrage to Geoffrey, communication broke down.*

A meeting was arranged with Petra, the Departmental Manager, where the initial feelings of both sides were explored and each was given an opportunity to express their frustrations. Elaine was angry since she felt her trust in Geoffrey had been betrayed because she had not been given enough information; she felt she had been misled. Geoffrey expressed his frustration at not being allowed to proceed with the project when he initially suggested it and also felt annoyed that he had to take Elaine's direction over his work.

Petra then encouraged some exploration of the facts of the case, over which there was some disagreement. Geoffrey insisted that he had at one point mentioned the project to Elaine, while Elaine denied this and said that despite weekly meetings with Geoffrey she had never received any information about the fact that he was pursuing the project.

Petra then explored some goals for the future. Both sides agreed on a need to communicate more about all aspects of work, particularly because Geoffrey felt that he did not know enough about what Elaine was doing on a day-to-day basis and felt it was important for him to know as a team member. Better communication between the two about all aspects of their work was therefore agreed as a useful goal at which to aim. An action plan was determined which involved both Geoffrey and Elaine meeting weekly to talk about the progress of the work and to update each other on activities. Geoffrey was firmly instructed not to engage in future activities without clear organizational sanction.

Assertive or mediation strategies are therefore necessary and useful approaches when conflict between team members is interfering with the well-being of the individuals or the effectiveness of the team. However, a note of caution is in order. There is sometimes a tendency for team members to wish to hold inquests over every small conflict which takes place within the team. This can have the effect of magnifying those inevitable but small differences which occur between team members on a day-to-day basis. Engaging in such focused, repeated and concentrated analyses can magnify conflicts and can be as detrimental to team functioning and individual mental health as avoiding discussion of conflicts altogether.

SUPPORT FOR TEAM MEMBER GROWTH AND DEVELOPMENT

Opportunities for learning, growth and development are of enormous importance to people's job satisfaction. Those who find themselves in mundane, monotonous, repetitive jobs are usually much less happy at work than those whose jobs are challenging and provide opportunities for new learning and development. The latter tend to be more committed to their jobs, their teams and their organizations and are consequently more productive.

The process of growth and development planning is used to enable people to assess themselves realistically, and then determine their skill, training and development needs. Team members can work together in planning ways of meeting their needs for growth and development and in providing feedback about skills and strengths. Such team-based growth and development planning also improves communication and understanding between team members, leading to shared understanding about needs, goals, values and strengths.

SKILL DEVELOPMENT
One way of beginning this process is for team members to list their own and others' strengths, skills and principal weaknesses. This enables the team both to ask and to answer important questions: What skills would team members like to develop further? Do team members have the opportunity to develop these skills in their current jobs? What professional or technical skills do team members want to develop further? How can the team get the training or support to enable its members to develop these skills? What support can the team offer to ensure individual team members get the training and development opportunities they want?

JOB ENRICHMENT
It is often useful for the team to consider how team members' roles can be enriched or enlarged to make them more fulfilling and satisfying. In particular, how could jobs within the team be changed to enable team members to achieve more of their goals, to align their jobs more appropriately with their values, interests and skills, and to provide opportunities for development, challenge and change? The content of team members' roles can be considered in six main areas: objectives and goals ; methods – how the job is done; scheduling – the order in which different parts of the job are done; relationships – who team members work with and how; location – where they work; innovation – introducing new and improved ways of doing things.

BALANCE BETWEEN HOME AND WORK LIFE
One of the mistakes that is sometimes made in relation to growth and development planning, is to separate one's work life out from the rest of one's life and to treat work as though it were somehow the only important part of life. In fact, we all have to find ways of integrating the demands of work life with the demands and needs that we have in our non-work lives. An intrinsic part of growth and development planning is considering personal goals and how to integrate these with work-related goals. The team can help in enabling or supporting the individual in finding a balance between home and work life.

A TEAM EXERCISE TO PROMOTE JOB ENRICHMENT

EXERCISE 7

A way of proceeding with job enrichment is to ask team members to help each other find answers to the following questions:

1. What would you add to or take out from your work objectives in order to enrich or enlarge your job?
   'I would add the chance to liaise directly with patients over their problems and requirements from the practice. The current method of feedback through comments sheets placed in the reception area creates too much formality and is an obstacle to direct communication.'

2. How would you change the methods that you use to achieve work objectives in order to enrich the job?
   'There would be much more communication within the team about the health of whole families, rather than just individuals within families in relation to treatment and care.'

3. How would you change the scheduling of the work that you do, i.e. the order in which different parts of the job are done in order to make the job more satisfying to you?
   'I would deal with medical records for just one hour in the morning and then write reports and do telephoning after that. I'd keep the afternoons free for meetings with other members of the team rather than do all these things jumbled up.'

4. Which individuals, groups or organizations would you work with more (or less) in order to enrich the job and make it more satisfying for you?
   'I would work more directly with the GPs and the counsellor in considering the needs of particular families or patients.'

5. In what ways would you liaise differently with the people with whom you work to make the job more satisfying for you?
   'I would like team members to take more initiative and share responsibility for team objectives so that I have less of a directive role as a GP.'

continued

continued —

6. In what areas of the job would you like the freedom and resources to introduce new and improved ways of doing things?
'I'd like to work in a smaller sub-team within the practice working solely on identifying new and improved ways of providing services for clients.'

Working with other team members to examine these issues from your particular standpoint makes job enrichment more possible than doing the exercise in isolation. Team members can then provide a socially supportive role in helping the individual find the time to get additional training in order to facilitate job enrichment.

SOCIAL CLIMATE

The general social climate of a team is a product both of team task processes described in previous chapters as well as the social processes described earlier in this chapter. There are some additional simple rules of intra-team conduct which can help the quality of overall relationships within the team such as the politeness of team members taking the time to greet each other in the morning; enquiring after the success of non-work events in colleagues' lives such as birthdays, weddings, holidays, etc. Taking the time to show interest and concern about the lives of others in the team is a simple and symbolic way of affirming relationships and caring – a kind of 'social grooming'. Other symbols of warmth and regard, commonly used in teams, are giving of birthday cards and celebrating the successes of individual team members.

In my work with health visitors, I met one team who would buy a cake once a week and share it at the end of their Friday afternoon working session. The 'squidgy cake' session became a potent symbol of mutual supportiveness in their work.

Another positive element in team social climate is *humour*. Non-aggressive humour is a rich source of positive feeling within the team, encouraging both closer team relationships and creativity. By developing a relaxed, enjoyable atmosphere team members are likely to be committed to the team and to enjoy their jobs. Humour is also a form of creative play which fosters an ethos of innovation within a team.

More formal approaches to promoting a positive team climate are also useful such as parties at team members' homes, shared activities such as fitness routines, jogging, football games (which involve both genders); and other sporting activities such as badminton, swimming etc. In the team within which I currently work, for example, some members play five-a-side football together at the gymnasium, while others swim or occasionally run together. Sometimes the whole team gets together at a social function or to attend a theatre production or jazz concert. At Christmas too, the team tends to go out together for a shared lunch. These events are clearly optional and are attended less by team members who have young families than those without. However, the ongoing, non-work related interactions promote relationships in the team which contribute to the overall social climate.

The message of this chapter is that the four social dimensions of team functioning (social support, conflict resolution, support for growth and development, and general social climate) influence the team's longer-term viability, but also impact upon the mental health and job satisfaction of individual team members. Psychologists may sometimes over-complicate what are relatively simple aspects of human behaviour and perhaps the most unguarded message of this chapter is that team members can help each other and themselves by caring for one another in the work setting. The message of all the major world religions is the same, that our purpose in any sphere of activity should be to care for those around us. The Dalai Lama expresses this simple principle in his repeated clear prescription: 'be kind to one another'. No less should this apply in the world of work.

Chapter Seven

Managing Teams

Difference of opinion leads to enquiry and enquiry to truth.
(Thomas Jefferson)

The hottest places in hell are reserved for those who, in time of great moral crisis, maintain their neutrality. (Dante)

Those involved in leading and managing teams need to exercise appropriate behaviours at the right times which requires a good deal of skill; for example, in timing the point at which they will intervene in a team's work in order to change direction, improve efficiency or change the structure of the team. Managing a team also requires a high level of interpersonal skill in giving clear direction, appropriate feedback and adequate support. A team leader must be an intelligent decision-maker since managing a team often involves working in situations of high ambiguity and uncertainty while making judgements about appropriate structures and processes within the team. Finally, the anxiety created by uncertainty and the conflict created by interpersonal difficulties between team members or with team leaders inevitably requires a good degree of emotional resilience.

Teams can play out many of the tensions and interactions which accompany family life and teams can even be seen to recapitulate the dynamics team members experienced in their families as children. Indeed there is a whole school of psychology centred on the Tavistock Institute of Human Relations which examines the extent to which work teams and organizations are characterized by the same dynamics as those which typify family life. Thus there are the tensions between dependence and independence, scapegoating and favouritism, and having one's own needs fulfilled versus satisfying the needs of others. For a manager or team leader these emotional and psychodynamic processes can create great tensions.

In this chapter, three overlapping approaches to structuring, supporting, guiding and directing team activities are explored:

1. Managing - objectives, roles and performance monitoring.

2. Coaching – managing day-to-day interactions and processes.

3. Leading – the long-term strategic view.

These three approaches to ensuring team effectiveness are necessary components of the team leader's or manager's work. Managing a team involves ensuring that objectives, team members' roles and team structures have been established and are regularly reviewed, also making certain that formal feedback about team performance is given to team members. Coaching is more to do with the facilitation and management of day-to-day team processes, involving an emphasis on listening rather than administering. Whereas managing focuses more formally on monitoring and feedback and communicating information about the wider organization, coaching is a less formal process, an internal role in which the coach listens, supports and offers advice, guidance and suggestions to team members. Finally, leading refers to the traditional notion of the leadership role, the process of making appropriate strategic interventions in order to motivate and give direction to the team. It involves ensuring that motivation remains high and that people are working as a team in a collaborative, supportive way and with a sense that the team has the ability and potency to accomplish its tasks. Leading involves intuition, fine judgement and risk. It may also demand external confidence and even charisma.

MANAGING A TEAM

WHAT ARE THE PRINCIPAL TASKS OF A MANAGER?

1. Setting clear shared objectives

This aspect of a team's functioning was explored in Chapter 2. The team has to ensure that a process of negotiating its objectives takes place, and this task usually falls to the manager. The manager must also ensure that there is some degree of consistency between organizational objectives and team objectives. A statement of those objectives must be laid down in a form that makes the work of the team clear both to itself and to others within the organization.

At the same time a manager must ensure that the team has an intrinsically interesting task to perform (see Chapter 1), because this will impact upon team motivation, commitment and effectiveness.

2. Changing the roles of team members

The manager must also ensure that the roles of individuals in the team are clarified both for the incumbents and for other team members. The analysis of team functioning in Chapter 1 indicated how important it is for team members to have roles which are clear, unique, important and tied in to team goals. It is important that each team role is, in part at least, unique to that person, important to the team's work, and contributes to the achievement of team objectives.

3. Developing individual tasks

For effective team functioning, individual roles and tasks should be seen by the incumbent as meaningful, whole pieces of work, giving them opportunities for growth and development and the exercise of skills. In order to maintain motivation, enthusiasm and commitment, people need intrinsically interesting tasks to perform which offer them opportunities for challenge, creativity and skill development. Part of the role of a manager is to enable individuals to set goals which stretch their skills, require new learning and are essentially interesting.

4. Evaluating individual contributions

The manager plays a central role in ensuring that individual contributions to overall team objectives are evaluated formally so that people have clear feedback on their performance. Such feedback is usually given on an annual basis, though more frequent feedback is valuable.

5. Providing feedback on team performance

The manager must ensure that the team as a whole receives feedback about its effectiveness, performance and overall contribution towards organizational objectives. This may involve the manager offering his or her subjective observations about the performance of the team, but should be based ideally on objective, quantitative and qualitative data wherever possible. It may also involve seeking feedback from those affected by the team's work.

For example, in a primary health care team, the manager might seek feedback in one of various forms: patient satisfaction surveys with the practice; patient satisfaction surveys with clinical interviews; feedback from relatives and carers on the supportiveness of the practice; feedback from local hospitals on the efficiency of the practice; or feedback from Social Services, Community Health Services and Family Health Service Authorities.

By fulfilling the role of gathering objective feedback, the manager provides the team with information about areas in which it is achieving its required targets and areas in which any discrepancies exist. The manager can then work with the team to set new standards and devise new procedures for achieving them. Too often teams are managed as though the individuals were simply working alone and performance feedback is given only at the individual level. Managers can contribute enormously to the promotion of effective team work and synergy by ensuring that frequent and clear feedback on performance is given to the team as a whole.

6. Reviewing group processes, strategies and objectives

There is growing evidence that a major contributor to effective team performance is 'task reflexivity.' Task reflexivity is the extent to which a team openly and actively reflects upon and appropriately modifies its objectives, strategies and processes in order to maximize effectiveness. In other words, teams should regularly take time out to review the methods, objectives and procedures they are using and modify them as appropriate.

Chris Argyris, an American organizational psychologist, has coined the term 'double loop learning' to describe the difference between how teams and organizations assess whether they are doing things right, versus whether they are doing the right things. Argyris argues that many organizations only consider how efficient they are, i.e., whether they are doing things right. For example, a manufacturer of metal springs might be spending more and more time focusing on whether the correct amount of tension exists within the springs that are being produced in order to achieve a bigger market. This is focusing on doing things right. However, double loop learning involves going a step beyond and asking whether the organization or team is doing the right thing. For example, it may be that the production of springs is not the right thing to be doing in a highly competitive market and that the manufacturer should change over to the production of nuts and bolts. In relation to health care, many teams might focus on how they can improve the quality of medical care given to patients who visit the surgery with complaints. However, an example of double loop learning is deciding to change the emphasis to health promotion rather than cure as a way of dealing with local health problems.

So, too, a manager can ensure that there is a high degree of double loop learning or reflexivity within a team by setting up regular reviews of team objectives, methods, structures and processes. As a minimum, in complex decision-making teams, reviews should take place at least every six months where the group discusses successes over the previous period, the difficulties encountered, as well as the failures of the team.

It is usually the responsibility of the team manager to set up 'time out' from the team's daily work to enable these review processes to take place. While some doubt the wisdom of taking time out from a team's busy work to conduct such reviews, there is strong evidence that teams which do this are far more effective than those which do not. Often in our work with the management teams of hospitals in the UK, we have found that teams under most pressure are those which are working least effectively and which are consequently least prepared to take time out to review their strategies and processes. It is as though they are running so fast on a treadmill, they are not aware of the opportunities that stepping off affords them, either to go in a different direction or to travel not on a treadmill but on an escalator!

COACHING A TEAM

Coaching means helping a team to achieve its objectives and its potential by giving frequent and specific support, encouragement, guidance and feedback. It is the process of facilitating the individual and collective efforts of members of a team. The team leader can perform this role in addition to the roles of managing and leading. The concept of coaching is based on the idea that there should be a mix of guidance in appropriate directions, along with creating the conditions within which team members can discover for themselves ways of improving work performance. Traditionally the former approach has tended to dominate amongst team managers and leaders, but increasingly evidence from within organizational and educational psychology suggests that the latter approach is more constructive.

1. LISTENING

It is characteristic of every book in this series of Personal and Professional Development that *listening* is a central element in coping with crises, managing stress, developing social skills and facing physical violence. Listening is the principal skill of team coaching. What are the elements of listening?

(a) Active listening

Active listening means putting effort into the listening process. All too often I am aware, when meeting with team members, how easy it is for me to be nodding, looking interested and concerned, but actually to be far away thinking about a previous meeting or, say, a conversation with my daughter. Active listening means giving active attention to the team member you are with here and now, as well as interpreting what they are saying, i.e. listening between the words.

(b) Open listening

Open listening is listening with an open mind; suspending judgement to let the individual work through an idea. The team coach should not assume he or she knows the answer before the person has told their story. Listening with an open mind involves suspending judgement until the person has had an opportunity to explore the issue thoroughly or to explain the issue fully to the team coach.

As discussed in Chapter 5, the best strategy for problem-solving is to spend most of the time clarifying the problem before trying to generate solutions. It is clearly not a productive course of action to generate solutions to the wrong problems! *The team coach should therefore encourage team members to explore problems fully rather than offering solutions.* This is very important and hard to practise in reality. For example, in working with hundreds of team managers across Europe who have role played team coaching, we have found the major challenge they experience is with the temptation to solve problems quickly. Coaching involves avoiding offering solutions to a problem that the coach has defined; rather it requires waiting until team members have clarified for themselves what the nature of the problem might be. It is not the role of a coach to offer solutions. It may be appropriate in certain leadership situations but it is not part of the coaching model.

(c) Drawing out

A major part of listening involves encouraging the individual to talk about his or her ideas, feelings and aspirations. This is helped considerably by asking what psychologists call 'open' questions, such as: Why?, How? and Who? The purpose is to enable people to elaborate and articulate their own exploration of a particular problem or issue which they are consulting the coach about. Closed questions are characterized by whether 'yes' and 'no' answers can be given in response to them, such as: 'Is spending too much time at work causing you problems at home in your relationship with your partner?' An appropriate open question in that situation might be: 'How is your current workload causing problems for you?' Again, most aspiring team coaches too readily identify the nature of the problem in their questioning. When a team member tells the coach that he is spending too much time at work, the coach may make the mistake of asking what appears to be an open question, but is in fact a closed and leading question such as: 'Why are you having difficulties prioritizing your work?' What a more effective team coach could ask is: 'Why do you think this is happening?' 'What sorts of pressures do you feel you are currently under?' 'How do you feel about it?'

(d) Reflective listening

Reflective listening involves re-stating your understanding of what a team member has said to you. Essentially it involves summarizing their previous statements, e.g.: 'So you're saying despite enjoying your work, you feel you want to have more freedom to define and pursue new projects on your own?' Again, this interpretation should not be the team coach's own definition of the nature of the problem, it should be a genuine attempt to re-state and summarize the information given by the team member. This is a very powerful form of coaching behaviour which enables the individual to explore particular issues in his or her team work more thoroughly. Reflective listening is powerful for the following reasons:

- It ensures that the team coach has to listen actively to what the team member is saying.

- It communicates to the team member a genuine desire by the team coach to understand what he or she is saying.

- It gives the team member the opportunity to correct mis-understandings on the part of the team coach.

- It enables the team coach to be confident that he or she has a correct understanding of what the team member is saying.

- It builds mutual empathy and understanding.

Some team coaches may be concerned that simply re-stating information offered by the team member will appear to be an empty, parrot-like process. However, research on interaction processes has demonstrated that such summarizing statements normally encourage the team member to elaborate further on the information already given, rather than simply affirming the correctness of what was said. Exploration is facilitated rather than curtailed by reflective listening.

2. RECOGNIZING AND REVEALING FEELINGS

If a team coach is to facilitate team members' work and experiences, it is very important that the whole person is encompassed and not just those elements which are perceived as comfortable to deal with. It is sometimes appropriate and necessary to spend time exploring and clarifying the feelings of team members if a team coach is to perform his or her task effectively. This also demands revealing one's own feelings and being comfortable and clear about doing that. A team coach may be the object of the frustration or anger or, alternatively, may feel frustrated and angry with team members themselves. Dealing with those feelings in an appropriate way, and at the right times, is an important part of the coaching process, especially when they interfere with effective team task performance.

What is not being suggested here is that team coaches should explore every nuance of team members' emotional reactions and frustrations. Where there are major 'feelings' issues team members should be given an opportunity to express and explore those feelings. Team members who are feeling overloaded and frustrated with their colleagues may need some space to express that frustration before they are able to analyse the balance of tasks and priorities currently facing them. It is often the case that by focusing on feelings the facts emerge, whereas when the focus is on facts the feelings remain hidden and unexpressed. The expression of such emotions has a useful impact not just on people's immediate well-being but also on their ability to deal with similar stresses in the future. This is a theme which is explored in other titles in this series where the same prescription is offered.

3. GIVING FEEDBACK

'Feedback' is a word like 'participation' – widely used in organizations but often misunderstood and rarely practised. Feedback involves giving clear reactions to specific behaviours in a sensitive and constructive way.

When Nigel Nicholson and I conducted a survey of over 2,000 British managers we found that most criticized their organizations for not giving them positive feedback about their work. When we then asked managers to analyse their own time use we found that they prioritized giving positive feedback to their own team members almost at the bottom of their list of activities!

Giving feedback as a team coach involves telling people about your observations of their behaviour and your observations of the consequences of their behaviour. For example: I noticed that you stopped the group from reaching agreement about the inclusion of that set of questions in the questionnaire because you had a sense that they were not appropriate. This was in the face of some frustration from other team members. However the consequence was that a much better set of questions was achieved and will provide us with more useful information as a result.

In this instance, feedback focuses on a particular example of behaviour and the positive consequences of it. Feedback is not about patting people on the head and giving them 'smiley faces.' That can be merely patronizing and implies the team coach has a parental type of power over the individual. Rather, feedback should be aimed at consolidating and improving performance within the team.

Feedback is most effective in changing and strengthening behaviour when it follows immediately after the behaviour. However, within organizations feedback is often withheld until the annual appraisal meeting. This has very limited impact on behaviour. The team coach should provide feedback for team members on a daily basis.

Positive feedback is much more effective in changing behaviour than negative feedback. It is better to ensure a very strong balance of positive against negative feedback. However, because we are quicker to recognize the discrepancies between actual and desired behaviour in the workplace, the balance is often inappropriately in favour of negative feedback. This is a consequence of our normal reaction to our environment. We tend to see discrepancy when what we expect and what actually occurs do not match.

Consequently the team coach has to work hard to find examples of consistency – when there is a match between expectations and reality – rather than discrepancy, and then to provide feedback as a result.

4. AGREEING GOALS

It is the superordinate task of a team leader, manager, or coach to help set direction and goals. It is a fundamental principle of work behaviour that goal setting has a powerful influence on performance. The role of the facilitator or coach in working with team members therefore must involve helping them to agree goals. If, for example, a team member is concerned about workload, part of the coaching should be to facilitate a shared agreement about goals between that team member and the coach. This may well involve setting goals for the team coach as well. These goals should be specific, measurable, achievable, relevant to the issue raised and time-based (see Chapter 2). Finally, and of equal importance, is ensuring that the team member and coach take action to ensure that the goals are achieved.

LEADING A TEAM

In contrast to managing and coaching, leading is a long-term strategic approach to managing a team. Leading refers to the less mechanical, perhaps more intuitive skills necessary for a team to find direction, synergy and success and it is to an examination of these skills that we now turn.

Over the last 15 years, Richard Hackman of Harvard University has studied a variety of team types including surgical teams, orchestras, cockpit teams, basketball teams and banking teams. His results suggest that there are three main functions of a team leader.

1. Creating favourable performance conditions for the team
This involves ensuring that the team task is well-defined; that the team has good organizational resources and clear boundaries. According to Hackman this will involve the team leader using his or her resources and authority or exercising influence laterally or upwardly within the organization to ensure that favourable performance conditions are created.

2. Building and maintaining the team as a performing unit

The team leader must ensure that the team has an appropriate mix of skills and abilities, but is nevertheless not so large that it cannot perform efficiently.

3. Coaching and helping the team

Hackman argues that a major function of team leadership is to coach and help the team on a day-to-day basis by making appropriate interventions and using some of the skills of coaching described in the previous section. This requires an ongoing sensitivity to patterns of interactions and processes of performance that are occurring within the team throughout its life-span.

TRIP-WIRES FOR TEAM LEADERS

Hackman has conceptualized some of the tasks of the team leader as trip-wires to be avoided. He defined five principal trip-wires:

1. Call the performing unit a team, but really manage members as individuals

There are two ways to manage a team. First, individual responsibilities can be assigned and then individual activities are conducted so that their efforts meet to form the whole team product. The second strategy is to assign a team task and give team members responsibility for determining how that task shall be completed.

Hackman argues that a mixed model, where people are told they are a team but are treated as individuals with individual performance appraisal and individual rewards, actually confuses the issue and leads to ineffectiveness in team performance. Individual performance is rewarded with bonuses but team performance is never attended to. Similarly, the careers of individual team members are managed separately and sometimes even in competition with one another. Consequently team working is inhibited since team members are likely to compete rather than co-operate with one another towards achieving shared goals.

To reap the benefits of team work, one must actually build a team. Calling a set of people a team or exhorting them to work together is insufficient. Instead, explicit action must be taken to establish the team's boundaries, to define the task as one for which members are

> *collectively responsible and accountable, and to give members the*
> *authority to manage both their internal processes and the team's*
> *relations with external entities such as clients and co-workers.*
>
> (Hackman, 1990, p. 495).

2. 'Fall off the authority balance beam'

Exercising authority in teams creates anxiety for team members and for team leaders. Inappropriate ways of resolving that anxiety are sometimes to exercise excessive leadership and sometimes to exercise too little. Leadership involves exercising authority in some areas and withholding it in others; or conversely, giving autonomy in some areas but withholding it in others.

Authority, for both psycho-dynamic and interpersonal reasons creates tensions for people within teams. Hackman argues that managers should be unapologetic about exercising authority to ensure that direction is achieved for the team's work, since this is such a fundamental contributor to team effectiveness. At the same time teams should be given the authority, within obvious boundaries, to determine the means by which they achieve their ends. Ensuring that the team has set itself a clear direction empowers rather than disempowers the team. One can 'fall off the authority balance beam' by giving a team too much autonomy or leeway by not providing sufficient direction; the result is that the team wallows in uncertainty and lacks motivation and commitment. Alternatively, the team leader can exercise too much authority and prevent the team from operating as a team altogether. A mistake that many team leaders make is giving a team too much authority early in its life when direction is needed and then intervening too heavily later when the team is not performing well.

3. Simply assemble a large group

Where group composition is unclear or vague and where structures and responsibilities have not been worked out, team members may fall victim to the kinds of process losses such as social loafing and free rider effects that were described earlier.

Hackman argues that three important elements are necessary to ensure a suitable structure for a team. First is a *well-designed team task* which represents a meaningful and motivating piece of work accompanied by a sufficient degree of autonomy for team members to be able to conduct the work successfully and get direct feedback about the results of their efforts.

Second is a *well-assembled team* which should be as small as possible while enabling the team to get the job done efficiently and which has the appropriate mix of skills and resources within the team. There is a good deal of evidence that with increasing group size, team effectiveness decreases. It is also suggested that the team members should not be too similar to one another since otherwise there may be a high degree of consensus, conformity and a low degree of creativity. At the same time, the team should not be composed of people of such dissimilar backgrounds, ages and views that team viability is threatened, i.e. team members become so unhappy in the situation that they leave the team early.

Third, the team should have *very clear, explicit and unambiguous information* about the extent and limits of its authority and account-ability so that team members do not stray into areas beyond their scope or make decisions which are not appropriate for them to make.

4. Specify challenging team objectives but skimp on organizational support

Teams in organizations are sometimes given 'stretch' objectives which require them to set ever more difficult targets. This can be very useful in improving performance and giving team members a sense of challenge. However, organizations sometimes give inade-quate organizational resources to enable teams to get their work done. The key resources are:

a *reward system* that recognizes and rewards excellent team perfor-mance not just individual performance;

an *educational system* within the organization that provides the necessary training in skills to enable the team to achieve its objectives;

an *information system* that provides the team with the kinds of data which will enable them to achieve their objectives and in an ade-quate form;

and the *material resources* which will enable them to get the work done, such as money, computing equipment, congenial space, staff, etc.

It is my observation that in many organizations there is little thought given to how teams rather than individuals can be rewarded or how teams can be provided with the resources and information that they need. This is despite the fact that team-based organizations are becoming much more the norm within both the public and private sectors. There is also very little training given to people for working in and managing teams despite the fact that teamwork is now considered such a basic building block of functioning organizations. Leaders must therefore work hard to exercise upward and lateral influence to ensure that appropriate support systems are available for teams within organizations.

> *The potential of a well-directed, well-structured, well-supported team is tremendous. Moreover, to stumble over the organizational support trip-wire is, perhaps, the saddest of all team failures. When a group is both excited about its work and all set up to execute it superbly, it is especially shattering to fail merely because the organizational supports required cannot be obtained. It is like being all dressed up and ready to go to the prom only to have the car break down en route.*
>
> (Hackman, 1990, p. 501)

5. Assume that members already have all the competence they need to work well as a team

Team leaders have to make process interventions to improve the effectiveness of teams from time to time. However, the point at which they intervene is very important also. Team leaders must take the time to coach and help team members and the team as a whole through periods of difficulty as well as through periods of success, and it is a mistake to assume that team members are competent to deal with new challenges as they come up. Team leadership involves constant awareness of the processes in teams and active intervention to improve them at appropriate times.

TIPS FOR SUCCESSFUL LEADERSHIP

Hackman points out three other noteworthy issues to do with team leadership, arguing that despite the fact that there is no preferred leadership style of democracy, authoritarianism, gentleness or extroversion, there are certain right and wrong directions.

1. The timing of leader interventions

Teams are much more responsive to leader interventions at the beginning of their life, or when they reach a natural break in their work, or when the 'product' has been produced or a performance period has ended. When a team is getting on with its work and is engaged in the process of doing the job intensively, it is generally a bad time for leader interventions since it disrupts the effectiveness of the group.

2. Coaching alone is insufficient

If a team is badly set up in the first place or does not have appropriate organizational support, coaching and similar process interventions are unlikely to have favourable effects upon group performance. If a team lacks direction, coaching alone may well not help.

3. Making a good start

What happens when the team first comes together and begins to work has an enduring impact upon subsequent performance. It is almost as though the seeds of the team's work determine its subsequent evolution. Therefore taking time to ensure an auspicious beginning to a team's life is valuable since the learning resources laid down at this point may have an important beneficial effect when a team encounters serious difficulties later on.

SELF-MANAGING OR SELF-LEADING WORK TEAMS

Much of the discussion in this chapter has implied that leadership, management or coaching is the remit of one member of the team. It is certainly more convenient to describe management and leadership in this way, but it is important for the reader to be aware that every member of the team should take some responsibility for managing, coaching and leading. These are not functions which should be exclusively assigned to one individual. If team members evade their own responsibilities for direction, support, influencing and authority in the team, it is likely that the team will be less effective. Managing meetings, for example, is the responsibility of each person in the team. When a team member sees the team going in what they think is an inappropriate direction, it is his or her responsibility to speak up if team effectiveness is to be maximized.

This chapter has examined the concepts of team management, team coaching and team leadership. It should be clear to the reader that there is no simple prescription for managing or leading teams. Being democratic or authoritarian, supportive or directive, hands-off or hands-on – are all necessary elements of the role of those leading the team. Much depends on the time in a team's life, the stage of the projects it is pursuing, the organizational context within which it is working, the individual personalities and skills of team members, and the personality of those delegated to be team leaders.

It has also been argued that team management, team coaching and team leadership are the responsibility of all team members and that responsibility should not abrogated in situations where one person is designated as team leader. The promise of effective managing, coaching and leadership is that the skills and abilities of diverse individuals can be moulded together to produce excellent team performance where the ideal of synergy is created in practice and not just in theory. As those who have worked in successful teams will know, the consequences in personal satisfaction, sense of competence and collegiality are enhanced considerably and the sense of being part of an effective dynamic unit is indeed a rewarding one.

Chapter Eight

Team Building

Parallel to the development of the team as a principal functional unit of organizations has come the development of a myriad of team building interventions offered by consultants, popular books and personnel specialists. However, recent reviews of the effectiveness of team building interventions have shown that, while they often have a reliable effect upon team members' attitudes to and perceptions of one another, there is little impact upon team task performance. How do we reconcile the contradiction between the increase in the number of team building interventions offered and the lack of evidence justifying their effectiveness?

It appears that most team building interventions focus on team relationships and cohesiveness, and are based on the mistaken assumption that improvements in cohesiveness lead to improvements in team task performance. In the few interventions which have focused primarily on task issues there does appear to be some improvement in task-related performance, though not consistently so. In this chapter a clear distinction is drawn between team task processes and team social processes.

As has been argued elsewhere in this book, team social processes are unlikely to affect team task processes unless there has been a major breakdown of relationships within the team. What is also emphasized is the value of clarifying the type of team building intervention required and then identifying very specific objectives, rather than assuming that a general intervention will have certain effects. Many team building interventions are based on the expectation that a day or two of team building will lead to dramatic improvements in team functioning. It is equivalent to hoping that one session of psychotherapy will change a person's life dramatically. The evidence suggests that it is continual interaction and effort which lead to improvements in functioning rather than any 'quick fix'.

TYPES OF TEAM BUILDING INTERVENTIONS

Team building interventions can be divided into five main types, each requiring a very different approach. Before beginning an intervention a team should therefore satisfy itself about the type of team building intervention required:

1. TEAM START-UP

This type of team building is specific to a team which is just beginning its work and which requires clarification of its objectives, strategies, processes and roles. The beginning of a team's life has a significant influence on its later development and effectiveness, especially when crises occur. Start-up interventions can help create team ethos, determine clarity of direction and shape team working practices. Many of the issues which should be dealt with in a start-up intervention were covered in Chapter 1. They include:

- Ensuring the team has a whole and meaningful task to perform.

- Clarifying team objectives.

- Ensuring that each team member has a whole, meaningful and intrinsically interesting task to perform.

- Ensuring that team members' activities can be evaluated.

- Ensuring that team performance as a whole is monitored and that team members are given regular and clear feedback on individual *and* team performance.

- Establishing a means for regular communication and review within the team.

It is ambitious to introduce established procedures in all areas of a team's functioning at its inception. Rather, effort should go into determining: the overall task and objectives for the team; clarifying objectives and inter-related roles for team members; building in performance feedback for individual team members and the team as a whole; and establishing mechanisms for regular communication and review of all aspects of team functioning.

2. REGULAR FORMAL REVIEWS

Formal reviews usually take the form of 'away days' of one or two days' duration during which the team reviews objectives, roles, strategies and processes in order to maintain and promote effective functioning.

As in any other area of human activity, regular review of functioning can lead to greater awareness of strengths, skills, weaknesses and problem areas, and future functioning being improved. Whether for individuals, couples, families, teams or organizations, there is value in stepping back from on-going day-to-day processes, examining areas of activity and reflecting upon the appropriateness of existing ways of doing things. Within work teams, regular away days are a useful way of ensuring a team's continuing effectiveness. Indeed there is much evidence that teams which take time out to review processes are more effective than those which do not.

When should a team take time out for an away day? When a team is involved in completing its work effectively and busy with task-related issues, an away day to review activities can be disruptive. A good time to schedule an away day is when a team has completed a major component of its work. However, if away days are regularly established, for example, on a six-monthly basis, then these need not interfere with the team's normal functioning since they are expected and can be used to deal with specific issues identified by the team. Away days should be of at least one full day's duration since there is usually more to talk about than is anticipated. Two days are ideal for most teams, but in some cases, this may be perceived as a luxury.

There is great advantage in conducting away days in comfortable locations away from the team's normal working environment. I have conducted team building sessions for BP Oil Europe in the luxurious Brussels Sodehotel in Belgium. However, the drawback was that the hotel was located a mere 200 metres from BP Oil Europe's headquarters and team members would sometimes 'slip out' to attend to an 'urgent' matter of business. It is therefore wise to hold team sessions well away from the demands of the place of work to avoid such interruptions. At the same time, there is much to be said for the kind of comfort and facilities provided in hotels and conference venues. Having a good supply of flip charts, pens, paper, post-it notes, good food and pleasant surroundings can make the team work enjoyable and pleasurable, especially for those who are reluctant initially. Both the financial commitment and the time invested in a well-conducted, focused away day is more than amply remunerated by the returns in performance which can accrue.

All team members should attend away days and, where possible, a facilitator should be commissioned. Facilitators enable team leaders and other team members to focus on the content of the day, without being distracted by responsibility for the processes. Also, a facilitator can sometimes provide an outside view of processes and comment on apparent diversions or blockages. Facilitators should be chosen with care. They should have experience of team interventions and be knowledgeable about team processes. Ideally the facilitator will be a chartered occupational psychologist who can provide evidence of team development work in other organizational settings and who would be prepared to give the names of contacts in organizations who could vouch for the effectiveness of their intervention work. The facilitator should have a good knowledge of the relevant research literature on groups at work. Finally, he or she should advise on how to evaluate the effectiveness of the interventions.

Away days must be carefully planned, but with a sufficient degree of flexibility to allow emerging topics to be dealt with appropriately. Having a well-structured programme of activities is essential for a productive away day. It is useful to have a mix of individual work, pairs work, syndicate work, and whole group work. Individual work is often necessary to enable team members to clarify their thoughts and reactions to various issues before being exposed to the melting pot of the whole group. Pairs work is an invaluable way of ensuring that all team members are encouraged to be active in the process of reviewing activities. It is also much less threatening for some team members than working in larger groups. Syndicate work involves small sub-groups of the team working together and this can encourage team members who do not normally work together to share their knowledge and expertise. Finally, whole group work is valuable in ensuring that the whole team has ownership of outcomes. It also minimizes suspicions about any secret deals and political manoeuvrings which might be taking place.

What topics or what content should be dealt with? There is little value in trying to cover every topic in one day. Changing behaviour is extremely difficult and trying to change complex teams in one session is nigh impossible. Away days should focus on a limited range of topics, such as objectives and communication. One indication that an away day intervention has attempted to cover too many areas is when the end of the day is rushed and action plans are ill-specified and badly formulated. Topics to be covered in an away day can include:

- Team successes and difficulties in the previous six-months or one-year period.

- A review of team objectives and their appropriateness.

- The roles of team members.

- Quality of team communication.

- Team interaction frequency.

- Team decision-making processes.

- Excellence in the team's work.

- Support for innovation.

- Team social support.

- Conflict resolution in the team.

- Support for personal growth and development.

3. *ADDRESSING KNOWN TASK-RELATED PROBLEMS*
In order to deal with specific known problem issues the team must take time out to define carefully the task-related problem it is confronting. Then the team develops alternative options for overcoming the problem, and action plans for implementing the selected way forward.

Where a specific problem can be identified and team members are satisfied they have correctly identified the nature of the problem and not simply a symptom of a deeper unresolved team issue, it is useful to take time out for focused intervention. The content and process of the intervention depends very much on the nature of the problem. If it is one to do with objectives, participation, commitment to excellence, or support for innovation, then the exercises described in Chapters 2–5 of this book can be used. If it concerns the social elements of team functioning, the material described in Chapter 6 should be employed. In some circumstances, however, the nature of the problem will require a facilitator to help the team.

— DEALING WITH A KNOWN PROBLEM —

Wendy was the Assistant Team Leader in a voluntary organization's personnel department. She wanted a team-building workshop because of problems of team divisiveness and hostility. After background briefing on the history of the team, its tenure and its constitution, questionnaires were given to team members asking them to indicate what they saw as the major barriers to team functioning. Examination of the responses revealed a strong sense of dissatisfaction with Wendy as a manager. Most team members described her as being overly directive, bureaucratic and inclined to have favourites. A number of team members also felt that she was guilty of talking behind their backs about supposed 'poor performance'. This, they claimed, had led to bad feeling on the part of both Wendy's favourites and those seen as her victims. Wendy was in her first management position and felt uncertain and anxious, which may have contributed to her directive style and tendency to reward and punish inappropriately.

A day was set aside for a team-building intervention to examine the team processes. Wendy failed to turn up, phoning in to say she was ill. Nevertheless, the team decided to address the issue and discussed how they should function on that day, given the complication of Wendy's non-attendance. It was generally agreed that back-biting and gossiping behind Wendy's back would merely accentuate the overall problem. Ground rules were therefore established and the team worked on ways of generalizing these ground rules for the day and how they might be applied to the team's functioning overall in the longer term, including areas such as respecting confidentiality, dealing with issues openly, not making personal attacks and developing strong respect and support. The team also identified some ambiguity about Wendy's role, vis-à-vis the role of the team leader. It was decided that this should be addressed in separate meetings between team members, the team leader and Wendy herself in order to clarify her role and draw on her strengths and skills so that she could be more supportive to team members. Team members agreed to set up a time also to brief Wendy fully on the work of the day and to outline suggested solutions.

In the above example, a known problem was handled by a team in ways which led to improvement in team relationships and functioning It was an indication of the success of the day that the whole team, including Wendy, decided subsequently to set up regular away days for the team in the future.

Sometimes the known problem need not concern internal team functioning. One team I worked with was responsible for the production of springs used by the Ford motor company. They were experiencing problems with rejection rates from Ford who informed them that the quality of their springs was not up to the standards required. A team meeting was set up to learn techniques of total quality management and continuous improvement from an expert. This led to changes in team objectives, strategies and processes which had a dramatic impact on quality. The team was subsequently promoted far up the list of Ford's accredited suppliers.

4. IDENTIFYING WHAT THE PROBLEMS ARE

Here the intervention focuses on the diagnosis of task-related problems. After the agreed identification of the nature of specific problems the team goes on to use appropriate strategies to overcome them in future.

When a team is functioning ineffectively, but it is unclear what is the nature of the problem, three alternatives are possible. The first involves group discussions to explore and clarify the nature of the problems. As indicated earlier, the amount of time spent exploring and clarifying problems is disproportionately more valuable than the time spent trying to solve them. Extended group discussions examining problem areas can lead to good problem identification. A second alternative is for team members to offer their ideas individually and privately about the nature of the problem in response to open-ended questions on short questionnaires. The third approach is to employ the questionnaire measure included in the appendix at the back of this book (see pages 120-123). This questionnaire, which has been used with a large number and wide variety of teams, is well validated and has excellent reliability. It can be used effectively as a diagnostic instrument to identify problems in team functioning and as an aid to identifying techniques associated with particular team problems. All members of a team should complete the questionnaire if the exercise is to be effective.

5. SOCIAL PROCESS INTERVENTIONS

Social interventions focus on interpersonal relationships, social support, team climate, support for growth and development of team members, and conflict resolution. They aim to promote a positive social climate and team member well-being.

SATISFACTION WITH TEAM SOCIAL PROCESSES

EXERCISE 8

	Yes, very definitely	Yes, but only somewhat	No, but only somewhat	No, definitely not
Does the team provide adequate levels of social support for its members?	1	2	3	4
Does the team have constructive, healthy approaches to conflict resolution?	1	2	3	4
Does the team have a generally warm and positive social climate?	1	2	3	4
Does the team provide adequate support for skill development, training and personal development of all its members?	1	2	3	4

Have the whole team discuss team scores on this questionnaire and discuss whether there is a need to improve any of those areas of team social functioning.

Team social process interventions should be employed where a team has unsatisfactory answers to one or more of the questions listed in Exercise 8. Interventions should focus on one area rather than attempting to accomplish change in all. If, for example, the main problem is a lack of social support in the team, one solution might be to train team members in simple co-counselling techniques where individuals undertake to give a partner in the team a set period of time – say half an hour or an hour every month – to discuss work-related problems. It is a mutual contract where both team members are provided with equal time at the same session and ensures that all team members get regular support. The basic techniques of co-counselling can be taught at an intervention or on a course.

If the problem relates more to support for growth and development the team might spend a day identifying each other's skill training or personal development needs and then action plan for how they could best provide the support to enable these needs to be met. General social climate problems can be addressed by asking team members to agree to simple behavioural rules for improving team functioning, such as arranging regular and varied social events. Again action planning and agreed contracting arrangements within the team can promote the likelihood that good intentions will be carried through. Finally, if the problem relates to a failure to resolve conflicts in a timely fashion, conflict resolution techniques based on the principles of assertiveness and ethical negotiation can be introduced.

ROLE CLARIFICATION AND NEGOTIATION

One potential problem in teams is lack of clarity about team roles. The steps in role clarification and negotiation are described more fully in Exercise 9.

What this chapter has emphasized is the need for teams to review their functioning on a regular basis. Where a team is low in task reflexivity it is necessary to address this failure of adaptability. Some fear that such questioning generates conflict and uncertainty about the team's direction. However, it is important to reassure team members that such reflexivity holds within it the seed of opportunity and greater effectiveness which can produce an enhanced sense of competence, confidence and greater aspirations amongst team members. Moreover, the research evidence on reflexivity has strongly suggested that teams which do reflect on strategies in this way are highly effective in long-term performance. Reflexivity should therefore not simply involve team building interventions, it should be part of the texture of the day-to-day life of the team.

ROLE NEGOTIATION EXERCISE

EXERCISE 9

Team members use mutual influence and negotiation in order to change team behaviours and improve team functioning.

Step 1

Each team member lists his or her objectives and principal activities on a piece of flip chart paper.

Step 2

Each piece of flip chart paper is hung on the wall around the room and team members examine each role.

Step 3

Under three headings on a piece of paper, each team member writes down what behaviours they would like that person to do less, do more, or maintain at the present level in their working relationship. For example, a receptionist might indicate that they want a particular GP to keep them informed more fully of plans for the coming month, in order that they are not inappropriately ignorant of the GP's movements. The receptionist may ask the GP not to check so often that patients' paperwork has been completed, since it feels like controlling rather than trusting their role. Finally he or she may ask the GP to sustain these attempts to involve the receptionist in decisions concerning the general running of the practice.

Each person signs their name after their requests for more, less or maintained behaviour.

Step 4

Pairs of individuals within the team then meet to examine the end result. The two negotiate together in order to reach agreement about the various requests. This is a highly participative step in the exercise and some teams may need help in managing the negotiation, especially if a particular pair is having difficulty reaching agreement.

Through role negotiation, the needs of individual roles are met more effectively and the functioning of individual members is dovetailed more into the objectives and needs of the team as a whole. This is a very powerful exercise which can enhance team functioning considerably, overcoming many of the problems of process loss and co-ordination described in Chapter 1.

The different approaches to team building interventions have been examined and it has been stressed that teams should adopt interventions appropriate to their particular purposes. The blanket approach to team building often employed is unlikely to be effective for most teams. The first question to ask is 'What intervention is most appropriate, for which teams, and at which point in time?' Then the following checklist can be used to ensure appropriate focus for the intervention:

1. Are the objectives of the intervention clear?
2. Is the intervention appropriate for the particular issues facing the team?
3. Is the intervention appropriately timed?
4. Does the intervention attempt to cover too many areas?
5. Are means for sustaining change built into the intervention?
6. Are facilitators employed who have the knowledge and skills required to conduct team building interventions?
7. Will clear action plans emerge as a result of the team building intervention?
8. Will regular reviews be instituted as a result of the team building intervention?

Chapter Nine

Teams in Organizations

Teams have been described primarily as though they were self-contained entities; but almost all work teams are part of larger organizations and what they do affects, and is affected by, the larger organization. To understand working in teams therefore requires an understanding of the ways in which teams and organizations interact.

TEAM WORK FOR EFFECTIVE ORGANIZATIONAL FUNCTIONING

Until the 1990s there had been little understanding of how teams related to their wider organizational settings. Deborah Ancona at the Massachusetts Institute of Technology and David Caldwell at Santa Clara University have explored how teams 'bridge the boundaries' i.e. how teams interact with their organizations as a whole. By studying teams in interaction with their organizations, Ancona and Caldwell identified three main strategies that teams use in managing their organizational environments:

(a) *Ambassadorial activities*
These involve communicating with and influencing senior management in order to promote the team's profile and to give senior management a picture of the team as effective, committed and innovative. The aim of ambassadorial activities is also to secure organizational resources and protect the team from excessive interference.

(b) Task co-ordinator activities

These aim at improving communication with other teams and departments. Rather than being characterized by vertical communication (as is the case with ambassadorial activity), task co-ordinator activities focus on co-ordination, negotiation and feedback horizontally, i.e. with departments and teams at the same organizational level. The aim is to manage work flow activities in a more co-ordinated way in order to achieve more effective performance through negotiation and via feedback with departments and teams.

In the case of, say, an oil company training team this would mean engaging in high levels of communication with functional departments in order to gain information about training needs. The training team would also negotiate with those other departments in order to specify training course prices, priorities and frequencies. By seeking constant feedback on the adequacy of the training they would also be in a better position to co-ordinate and negotiate in the future.

(c) Scouting activities

These aim to provide the group with up-to-date information on market needs and requirements and on new technical developments. The aim of scouting activities is to be aware of changes occurring in the external environment of the team. One example comes from a research team established to examine the factors which contributed to the performance of manufacturing firms. One team member contacted other researchers on a regular basis to find out about new developments in the area, perused relevant journals to glean information about new methodologies, and consulted with academic contacts about related research. Such scouting activities provide a means of ensuring that a team is up-to-date with technical developments. This same team member also consulted with senior managers in other similar organizations to discover their principal questions about company performance in order that market needs for the research could be identified correctly.

Not all teams have a single dominant strategy for external activity within the organization. Some employ all three types of activities, while others focus on only one. Still others are isolationist, employing none of the strategies in any consistent way. What is fascinating about the results from Ancona and Caldwell's research is that team performance was not dependent upon the *level* of organizational communication that teams maintained. Far more important was the *type* of activities they engaged in. They found that teams which engaged predominantly in scouting activities had poorer performance than other teams. Moreover, internal processes within the team tended to be unsatisfactory. Task performance and team cohesiveness were both lowest in teams which adopted predominantly scouting activity strategies. In contrast, teams which adopted a 'comprehensive strategy' of a mix of ambassadorial, task co-ordinator, and scouting activities tended to have the highest performance, task process and team cohesiveness scores.

In the short term, ambassadorial activities were associated with the best team performance, good task processes and high cohesiveness. But over the long term a combination of ambassadorial and task co-ordinator external activities appears to be important. Comprehensive strategy teams were the most effective overall, though they seemed to pay a price with the cohesiveness of the team compared with the pure ambassadorial strategy teams.

Isolationist teams tended to do badly, though unlike the scouting teams, they did have higher scores on internal task processes and cohesiveness. It may be that these teams concentrated so much on internal processes that they neglected important organizational cues and so performed less well. Teams which engaged predominantly in scouting seemed to make their work so complex that they were unable to perform effectively. By seeking ever new approaches, they were unable to adopt a single team plan which took them forward over any period of time. No clear decisions were made about work plans or processes and no plan was ever effectively implemented. Continual external exploration brings conflicting information, requiring complex internal interaction. As the difficulty of decision-making becomes greater, relationships within the team suffer.

This research shows that, contrary to popular belief, it is not the amount of external communication that a team engages in which predicts successful team performance. Rather it is the *type* of external communication. Ancona and Caldwell's results can be used by all teams interested in improving their performance as a way of checking on the effectiveness of their own strategies within their organizations.

WHAT DO TEAMS NEED FROM THEIR ORGANIZATIONS?

Hackman and his colleagues at Harvard University have concluded that there are six principal areas within which teams need organizational support: targets, resources, information, education, feedback and technical/process assistance in functioning. Examining the extent to which organizations provide team support in these areas can help in discovering the underlying causes of team difficulties.

(a) Targets
Teams need support from an organization in determining targets or objectives. Surprisingly few teams are given clear targets by their organizations often because organizational targets and aims have not been clarified sufficiently. It is striking, when team members are asked to outline their objectives and team targets how few have clear notions of what is required of them. There is an implication that teams should derive their targets and objectives by scrutinizing the organizational objectives or mission statements. However, these are often such vague good intentions or positive but abstract sentiments that it is almost impossible for a team to derive clear targets and objectives. Where, through a process of negotiation, teams are able to determine their targets in consultation and collaboration with those hierarchically above them, there is usually a better level of performance.

(b) Resources
The organization is required to provide adequate resources to enable the team to achieve its targets or objectives. Resources include: having the right number and skill mix of people; adequate financial resources to enable effective functioning; may include secretarial or administrative support; adequate accommodation; adequate technical assistance and support (such as computers, blood pressure testing equipment, or appropriate equipment for testing infants' hearing, etc).

The research team which I lead has been conducting day-long interviews in manufacturing firms all over the UK for some time. Three team members are frequently travelling, staying overnight in hotels and interviewing senior managers in organizations. In order to sustain this high level of demanding activity they need specific resources: an adequate travelling expenses budget; an administrator back in the office who can handle phone calls and their travel and accommodation arrangements; lap-top computers and tape recording equipment to enable them to carry on their work while they are away. This highly effective team would almost certainly be less effective, and much less committed to this very difficult work, were they not supported by good resources from the research institute.

(c) Information

Teams need information from the organization which will enable them to achieve their targets and objectives. Changes in strategy or policy which are not communicated to teams can hamper their effective functioning. Ensuring that relevant information reaches a team to enable it to perform effectively is an essential component of an organization's management. For example, GPs need to provide health visitors with ready access to age/sex registers, medical records and other information about the practice population, in order for the health visitors to function effectively within the teams. Or an oil company which has decided to develop large numbers of international teams with team members based in different countries, has to communicate these policies and decisions to its training department in order that they can implement training which will facilitate the effective functioning of cross-cultural teams.

(d) Education

Part of an organization's responsibilities for effective team functioning is to provide the appropriate levels and content of education for staff within teams. The purpose of such training and education is to enable team members to contribute most effectively to team functioning and to develop as individuals. This includes on-the-job training, coaching via supervisor, training courses, residential training courses or distance learning courses. There should be adequate access to training which is relevant to the team's work and of a sufficient quality and quantity to enable them to perform to maximum effectiveness.

(e) Feedback

Teams require timely and appropriate organizational feedback on their performance if they are to function effectively. Timely feedback means that it occurs as soon as possible after the team has performed its task, or occurs sufficiently regularly to enable the team to correct inappropriate practices or procedures. Appropriate feedback means that it is accurate and gives a clear picture of team performance.

For some teams it is difficult to gain accurate feedback. For example, primary health care teams have almost no feedback at all. For a football team, feedback is immediate and is not dependant upon an organization, i.e. match results are evident on a weekly basis. For a team responsible for providing training in one division of, say, a major oil company, organizational feedback might take the form of senior managers' satisfaction with improved performance. This could include measuring the results from technical training courses in customer service in retail outlets (i.e. filling stations). Such information could come from surveys of customer satisfaction with retail operators' services.

Clearly there are large differences in the extent to which organizations can and do provide feedback to teams, but the aim should be for the organization to improve continuously in the extent to which it provides useful, accurate and timely feedback.

(f) Technical and process assistance
Teams need their organizations to provide the specialized knowledge and support which will enable them to perform their work effectively. A primary health care team engaged in developing its practice objectives, by identifying the health needs of the practice population, might need the health authority to deploy a community medical officer to advise the team on patterns in local health and ill-health. For a training team in an oil company, technical assistance might take the form of specialist computing experts and marketing strategists, advising the company on how to communicate most effectively to managers throughout Europe, in order to market their training courses to managers in different functions.

Process assistance refers to the organizational help available when team process problems are encountered. Are consultants and facilitators available to help the team identify, diagnose and overcome problems of team functioning from time to time?

WHAT DO ORGANIZATIONS REQUIRE FROM TEAMS?

Organizations need teams to set and then achieve objectives which enable the organization to achieve its own targets and goals. A Family Health Services Authority or District Health Authority, for example, will require their primary health care teams to meet the health needs of the local population. The training team in an oil company, on the other hand, may be required to identify carefully training needs and respond to them strategically in order that the organization can achieve its overall objectives via the improved individual performance of employees.

Co-operation between groups is required by organizations, even when they are competing for office space, resources or staff. Competing teams may deliberately deceive one another or try to hamper one another's performance. When teams co-operate within organizations, not only are organizational objectives better achieved, but individual team performance is also improved. The notion that competition between teams within organizations results in better performance is not well supported by research evidence.

An increasingly common phenomenon within organizations is the use of cross-functional groups. These are combinations of people from different teams who come together to improve communication and decision-making. For example, in a company which manufactures springs for the automotive industry, cross-functional groups may draw individuals from production, marketing, sales and customer liaison in order to identify and overcome quality and performance problems. Such cross-functional groups are increasingly seen as a way of addressing quality problems in the manufacturing sector and of ensuring better cross-team communication, co-ordination and co-operation. Such cross-team collaboration and communication fosters high levels of creativity and innovation within organizational settings.

HOW TO BE A REVOLUTIONARY TEAM

So far we have considered teams as though their objectives and those of the organization are consistent rather than in conflict. But it is also necessary to examine the situation in which an organization and team's objectives are not consistent.

In the UK National Health Service in the 1990s, this situation is not unusual. Many community nursing and hospital teams consider their objectives to be opposed to those of their management boards. A surgical team might feel that the managerial emphasis on cost cutting and reduction of waiting list times has jeopardized the quality of care available to patients. The management group, in contrast, might argue for the importance of setting priorities in treatment since they have a limited budget with which to provide surgical care.

The oil company training team might oppose senior management's strategy of 'macho' management which emphasizes increasing employee insecurity, while imposing compulsory redundancies and new contracts. The training team, in conjunction with personnel, might wish to oppose this policy and bring about organizational change. How is this to be done?

In Chapter 4, the literature on 'minority influence' was examined and this showed how minorities, by being persistent and consistent in the face of opposition, can bring about a subtle conversion of attitudes amongst majorities. This research has demonstrated convincingly how a well-organized minority may alter the thinking of a majority. The research also helps partly to explain how groups which start out as minorities, such as feminist or ecological movements, or the movement for the ordination of women in the Church of England, subsequently may bring about shifts in thinking, behaviour and even national policies. Serge Moscovici, who pioneered research and theory in this area, has argued that innovation can only come about through the conflict created by minority influence.

How can a team draw on this understanding in order to change organizational objectives and strategy? Based on our understanding of minority influence processes, the following guidelines can be offered:

(a) The team must have a clear vision of what it wishes to achieve
For example, a personnel department may have developed a major commitment to the implementation of equal opportunities on a real rather than cosmetic organizational basis. Opposition from senior management may exist but as long as the team has a shared vision of equal opportunities for women, ethnic minority groups, and the disabled, they have a chance of success. In order to be effective and to sustain minority influence, the vision must be one which motivates and inspires team members – a future they really feel is worth fighting for.

(b) The vision must be clearly articulated and coherently expressed
In order to be effective, minorities must put across a clear, consistent message backed up by convincing underlying arguments. A team in which the minority vision is unanimously held and consistently argued for is many times more effective than an

individual working alone – indeed it is exponentially more effective. Team members must present the same vision and the same arguments in favour of the vision. Where disagreement exists amongst members of a minority group they are not so effective in influencing the views of the majority and bringing about real change.

(c) *They must be flexible in responding to the views of others*
Minorities which are perceived to be radical and inflexible tend to be rejected by the majority as too extreme to bargain with. It is important for a minority to appear willing to listen to the views of others and make modifications to their proposals, while not fundamentally distorting their vision. The personnel department has to be prepared to listen to senior managers who argue that, say, introducing large numbers of untrained people very quickly into the organization may have a detrimental effect upon performance, or that any equal opportunities strategy should be managed in stages. Failure to respond to apparently reasonable arguments can cause the minority to be dismissed. However, this should not involve a team compromising its fundamental objectives.

(d) *Persistence is essential*
For a team to bring about organizational change it must be persistent. Minority movements such as the feminists and ecological campaigns had influence partly as a result of the repeated presentation of the same coherent message and the same arguments. Minority influence occurs as a result of persistent communication. Where a team is defeated in a committee or in some managerial decision-making process, it should not give up but should maintain its stance and either go back to the same decision-making bodies or find alternative routes to influence the organization. Presenting the same message persistently across the organization is likely to have the effect of water dripping on a stone: eventually the stone will begin to be worn away. In short the message is, *prepare, rehearse, present, and present again*. In other words, the vision and arguments for the team's position should be prepared and rehearsed in private and then the team should repeatedly present its approach to people throughout the organization. *Don't give up!*

(e) *Participation*
The single best way of reducing resistance to change is by involving people in the change process. By seeking the views of people

throughout the organization and encouraging others to be involved in contributing ideas to the proposals, the team can reduce the resistance of people in the organization to the proposed change.

(f) The bad news

An inevitable consequence of acting as an agent for revolutionary change is that the team increases organizational conflict. Repeatedly challenging organizational objectives or practices inevitably provokes conflict, often with people in higher status positions who have greater power. This is very threatening and deters many teams from engaging in revolutionary change processes. However, if a vision is worth fighting for, then team members will be prepared for the conflict which ensues. Such revolutionary approaches to organizational change also bring with them unpopularity. The majority in organizations tend to conform because it makes for a more peaceful life. Those who introduce conflict are likely to become unpopular since they raise anxiety. However, if the vision is really that important to a team – for example, in the case of a hospital nursing team, improving the quality of health of those in their care – team members may be prepared to tolerate unpopularity or even job insecurity as the price to be paid for that vision of a better world.

Such revolutionary teams may seem a threat to organizations. However, there is good reason for supposing that organizations which have no revolutionary teams are becoming stagnant, since the forces for change, conflict and innovation have been dampened down by conformity processes. *Organizations need revolutionary teams just as they need people with vision. It is only through the friction created by sharply differing views within organizations that heat is produced to fire creative and innovative processes.*

Teams within organizations are required to meet objectives which further organizational aims. In order to do this they need organizational support and resources such as information, training, accommodation, equipment and managerial support. But organizations are political entities characterized by conflicting interests, goals and agendas, and teams must manage this environment effectively in order to survive. They must develop strategies which raise the team's profile with senior management and win resources, which co-ordinate their efforts with those of other teams and departments, and which monitor the environment to ensure they are up to date with 'market needs' and new technical developments.

In some circumstances team members may be opposed to organizational objectives and changes. In order to change the organization, revolutionary approaches may be required based on developing a coherent vision and evoking that vision persistently for others in the organization. This is a strategy which uses conflict as a vehicle for innovation. To ensure long-term effectiveness, all teams should develop and sustain an evolutionary approach to their work, especially in changeable, uncertain environments. This involves regular reflection on the team's work and purpose, along with appropriate modification of activities and aims. Ultimately, team success and effectiveness is constrained or enhanced by the intelligence and integrity in its dealings with the wider organization.

CONCLUSIONS

Three themes have repeatedly emerged in this book, intersecting to form a single repeated pattern. First, in today's highly uncertain organizations characterized by high levels of work demands and rapidly changing structures and cultures, performance can be enhanced by team members taking time away to reflect quietly upon their functioning. This allows them to adapt courageously in order to achieve new evolutionary forms which fit their circumstances better. Secondly, teams need to find creative ways of working which challenge existing orthodoxies and offer alternatives to the status quo if they are to contribute substantially to organizational and societal development. Such creativity only comes from constructive conflict, and a preparedness to tolerate and even encourage uncertainty and ambiguity. In this way, those who work in teams can experience the excitement and mutual appreciation generated by real breakthroughs as a result of human collaboration. Thirdly, in demanding, changing, and uncertain environments people must support one another to create climates of safety, confidence and empowerment.

If the motivation and commitment of people are to be engaged in the work of their teams, there must be a strong sense of the value of the work they do. This may be in promoting health, conserving the environment, helping others to learn, supporting those in need, producing high quality goods for people, ensuring safety, promoting understanding, confronting injustice or contributing to the community. Vision is derived from values and our values determine our motivation. Reflexivity helps to clarify for team members the values they hold about both team social functioning and task performance. Such focus and clarity may also make salient the differences between team members' views and those of senior management or the organization as a whole. This in turn may lead to conflict. But such conflict is necessary for organizational adaptability and survival ensures that organizations reflect rather than eclipse the diversity of values in society. Through the development of evolutionary and revolutionary reflective teams described earlier, rather than society serving organizations, organizations may come to serve more fruitfully the societies of which they are a part.

Questionnaire

Date: _____

Team: _____

Instructions

This questionnaire asks about the climate or atmosphere in your work group or team. It asks about how people tend to work together in your team, how frequently you interact, the team's aims and objectives, and how much practical support and assistance is given towards the implementation of new and improved ways of doing things. There is no 'right' or 'wrong' answers to any of the questions – it is more important that you give an accurate and honest response to each question. Do not spend too long on any one question. First reactions are usually best. For each question consider how your team *tends in general to be* or *how you feel in general* about the climate within your team. Please circle your chosen answers using a ball point pen.

Part I   Communication and Innovation

	Strongly disagree	Disagree	Neither agree nor disagree	Agree	Strongly agree
1. We share information generally in the team rather than keeping it to ourselves.	1	2	3	4	5
2. Assistance in developing new ideas is readily available.	1	2	3	4	5
3. We all influence each other.	1	2	3	4	5
4. The team always functions to the best of its capability.	1	2	3	4	5
5. We keep in regular contact with each other.	1	2	3	4	5
6. In this team we take the time needed to develop new ideas.	1	2	3	4	5
7. People feel understood and accepted by each other.	1	2	3	4	5
8. Everyone's view is listened to, even if it is in a minority.	1	2	3	4	5
9. People in the team never feel tense with one another.	1	2	3	4	5
10. The team is open and responsive to change.	1	2	3	4	5
11. People in the team co-operate in order to help develop and apply new ideas.	1	2	3	4	5
12. Being part of this team is the most important thing at work for team members.	1	2	3	4	5

	Strongly disagree	Disagree	Neither agree nor disagree	Agree	Strongly agree
13. We have a 'we are in it together' attitude.	1	2	3	4	5
14. We interact frequently.	1	2	3	4	5
15. The team is significantly better than any other in its field.	1	2	3	4	5
16. People keep each other informed about work-related issues in the team.	1	2	3	4	5
17. Members of the team provide and share resources to help in the application of new ideas.	1	2	3	4	5
18. There are consistently harmonious relationships between people in the team.	1	2	3	4	5
19. There is a lot of give and take.	1	2	3	4	5
20. We keep in touch with each other as a team.	1	2	3	4	5
21. People in this team are always searching for fresh, new ways of looking at problems.	1	2	3	4	5
22. The team consistently achieves the highest targets with ease.	1	2	3	4	5
23. There are real attempts to share information throughout the team.	1	2	3	4	5
24. This team is always moving towards the development of new answers.	1	2	3	4	5
25. Team members provide practical support for new ideas and their application.	1	2	3	4	5
26. Members of the team meet frequently to talk both formally and informally.	1	2	3	4	5

Part II Objectives

	Not at all		Somewhat		Completely
27. How clear are you about what your team objectives are?	1	2	3	4	5
28. To what extent do you think they are useful and appropriate objectives?	1	2	3	4	5
29. How far are you in agreement with these objectives?	1	2	3	4	5
30. To what extent do you think other team members agree with these objectives?	1	2	3	4	5

	Not at all		Somewhat		Completely
31. To what extent do you think your team's objectives are clearly understood by other members of the team?	1	2	3	4	5
32. To what extent do you think your team's objectives can actually be achieved?	1	2	3	4	5
33. How worthwhile do you think these objectives are to you?	1	2	3	4	5
34. How worthwhile do you think these objectives are to the organization?	1	2	3	4	5
35. How worthwhile do you think these objectives are to the wider society?	1	2	3	4	5
36. To what extent do you think these objectives are realistic and can be attained?	1	2	3	4	5
37. To what extent do you think members of your team are committed to these objectives?	1	2	3	4	5

Part III Task Style	To a very little extent		To some extent		To a very great extent
38. Do your team colleagues provide useful ideas and practical help to enable you to do the job to the best of your ability?	1	2	3	4	5
39. Do you and your colleagues monitor each other so as to maintain a higher standard of work?	1	2	3	4	5
40. Are team members prepared to question the basis of what the team is doing?	1	2	3	4	5
41. Does the team critically appraise potential weaknesses in what it is doing in order to achieve the best possible outcome?	1	2	3	4	5
42. Do members of the team build on each other's ideas in order to achieve the best possible outcome?	1	2	3	4	5
43. Is there a real concern among team members that the team should achieve the highest standards of performance?	1	2	3	4	5
44. Does the team have clear criteria which members try to meet in order to achieve excellence as a team?	1	2	3	4	5

BIBLIOGRAPHY

Ancona, D. G. and Caldwell, D. F. (1992). Bridging the boundary: External activity and performance in organizational teams. *Administrative Science Quarterly*, 37, 634–665.

Anderson, N., Hardy, G. and West, M. (1990). Innovative Teams at Work. *Personnel Management*, Vol 22, 48–53.

Anderson, N. and West, M. A. (1994). *The Team Climate Inventory: Manual and User's Guide*. Windsor: ASE Press.

Belbin, R. M. (1981). *Management Teams: Why They Succeed or Fail*. London: Heinemann.

Belbin, R. M. (1993). *Team Roles at Work: A Strategy for Human Resource Management*. Oxford: Butterworth Heinemann.

Brown, R. (1986). *Group Processes*. Oxford: Basil Blackwell.

Buzan, T. (1974). *Use Your Head*. London: BBC Books.

Edelmann, R. (1993). *Interpersonal Conflicts at Work*. Leicester: BPS Books.

Egan, G. (1986). *The Skilled Helper*. 3rd Edition. California: Brooks Cole.

Fontana, D. (1989). *Managing Stress*. London: BPS Books and Routledge.

French, W. L. and Bell, C. H. (1978). *Organization Development: Behavioral Science Interventions for Organization Improvement*. New Jersey: Prentice Hall.

Guzzo, R. A. and Shea, G. P. (1992). Group performance and intergroup relations. In M.D. Dunnette and L. M. Hough (Eds). *Handbook of Industrial and Organizational Psychology*. 2nd Edition. California: Consulting Psychologists Press Inc.

Hackman, J. R. (Ed.) (1990). *Groups That Work (and those that don't): Conditions for Effective Teamwork*. San Francisco: Jossey Bass.

Handy, C. B. (1988). *Understanding Organizations (3rd Edition)*. Middlesex, England: Penguin.

Harvey, D. F. and Brown, D. R. (1988). *An Experiential Approach to Organizational Development. (3rd Edition)*. New Jersey: Prentice Hall.

Henry, J. (Ed.) (1991). *Creative Management*. London: Sage

Henry, J. and Walker, D. (Eds) (1991). *Managing Innovation*. London: Sage.

Janis, I. L. (1982). *Groupthink: Psychological Studies of Policy Decisions and Fiascoes*. Boston, Massachusetts: Houghton Mifflin.

Kanter, R. M. (1983). *The Change Masters*. New York: Simon and Schuster.

Makin, P., Cooper, C. and Cox, C. (1989). *Managing People at Work*. London: BPS Books and Routledge.

Milgram, S. (1974). *Obedience to Authority*. New York: Harper and Row. London: Tavistock Publications.

Morgan, G. (1986). *Images of Organization*. London: Sage.

Moscovici, S. (1976). *Social Influence and Social Change*. London: Academic Press.

Nicholson, N. and West, M. A. (1988). *Managerial Job Change: Men and Women in Transition*. Cambridge: Cambridge University Press.

Parry, G. (1990). *Coping with Crises*. London: BPS Books and Routledge.

Poulton, B. C. and West, M. A. (1994). Primary health care team effectiveness: Developing a constituency approach. *Health and Social Care*, 2, 77–84.

Reddy, M. (1987). *The Manager's Guide to Counselling at Work*. London: BPS Books and Methuen.

Rogelberg, S. G., Barnes-Farrell, J. L. and Lower, C. A. (1992). The stepladder technique: An alternative group structure facilitating effective group decision-making. *Journal of Applied Psychology*, 77, 730–737.

Tjosvold, D. (1991). *Team Organisation: An Enduring Competitive Advantage*. Chichester: John Wiley and Sons.

Vernon, P. E. (Ed.) (1970). *Creativity*. Middlesex, England: Penguin.

West, M. A. and Farr, J. L. (1990). *Innovation and Creativity at Work: Psychological and Organizational Strategies*. Chichester: John Wiley & Sons.

INDEX